In Praise of *How To Keep Your*

A compelling read for anyone who is serious about keeping their job. I also recommend it to anyone currently unemployed because once they get a new job this book will help them to keep it. "It can take 6 – 18 months to find a new job so it makes sense to invest time and energy in the one we have," says Richard Maun. This is so true, and following the practical advice and tips in this book will generate positive energy so people can start enjoying their job again. Asking oneself 'Am I value for money?' or 'Would I employ me?' is a huge wake-up call – how many people, before reading this book, have really asked themselves those questions?

Julie Bishop, Founder, www.JobHop.co.uk

A must read for all employees! Useful tips and practical activities make this one for everyone's collection. With this book, everyone can succeed in the workplace! Read it now and don't look back!

Kevin Bennett, Manager – Business Excellence, South West TAFE, Australia

If you think you know it all – you don't, until you've read this book. Richard's calm, structured, non-judgemental approach focuses on the key issues that provide a foundation and a framework that allow to you develop and grow. Upsizing, just as downsizing, can challenge you to keep your job and Richard delivers practical, fun techniques and approaches that encourage you to plan, prioritise and choose to change – to become a more effective, motivated and happier employee.

David Clover, Chief Business Development Officer, EV Offshore Ltd and EVO Inc, UK & USA

What a great book! Once again Richard has hit the nail on the head, providing real insights into the sometimes brutal, modern day working environment. The reality and perspective about decision making and how employees are perceived is bang on and is rarely committed to print. Richard highlights exactly the whys and hows of getting ahead at work, and as ever the useful tips, support and guidance can be used in many areas of life. Trust Richard to tell you exactly how it is, and then give you the tool box to manage yourself to employment happiness. I wish he had written this 10 years ago. Genuinely refreshing!

Jordan Dudley, Director, Dudley Child Recruitment Ltd, UK

A refreshingly straightforward book! It shows you how you can be more successful at work and defines success as being recognised as a productive and therefore valuable employee. In simple, pragmatic terms it shows how making a few changes in your own behaviour, taking actions that are within your control and using simple tools to manage your personal effectiveness can improve your value to an employer. The book shows you what to do, why you need to do it, and how to get started. With job security hard to come by, I can think of many people who would benefit from reading this book!

Geoff Nelder, former Director, Fellowship and Enterprise Centre,
Cranfield University, UK

Perfect for anyone who is worried about keeping their job or moving up the career ladder. Read this book, and you will gain skills and confidence that will stay with you for life. I have read and re-read all Richard's books. Why have I re-read them? Because they are so good! Richard provides grounded, practical advice – that you can use day in, day out, to make real changes.

Sara Greenfield, co-Owner, www.thebestof.co.uk/norwich

Anyone who spends most of their waking life in a working environment needs to read this book. In whatever business we operate we all feel better about ourselves if we believe that we are making a difference. For all sorts of reasons we hit barriers, they may just be temporary blockages on a project, or an employee relationship, or the 'big one' experienced by the character "Peter". At a time when we may feel disempowered and vulnerable, Richard from first-hand experience offers practical tools (the 4-hour list is a cracker) and great examples, to help us feel confident and resourceful.

Tony Hall, Chief Executive, Freebridge Community Housing, UK

Full of ideas on how to think differently about your job. This book will not only help you plan a strategy for survival in the workplace but will help you to plan a career. Valuable and thought provoking, the book allows the reader to seriously take stock of their position and then take positive steps to reduce stress and keep earning money!

David Dawber, CEO, Cliffe Packaging Ltd, UK

About the Author

Richard Maun facilitates personal and organisational development through executive coaching, management consultancy, interactive workshops and lively conference speaking. He specialises in using Transactional Analysis in organisational settings and combines it with Lean Thinking. He has worked with a wide variety of people in the public and private sector to help them act in awareness, improve team dynamics, increase leadership skills, refine business-related processes and keep their job.

Richard now runs his own management development company and is a director of a training company as well as a visiting lecturer at a leading UK university. He also works as a freelance business writer and has published three books with Marshall Cavendish – *Job Hunting 3.0*, *My Boss is a B@$T@*D* and *Leave The B@$T@*DS Behind* – that look at how to get a job in a competitive world, how to survive turmoil at work and how to set oneself up in business. All three are based on real-life experiences and contain practical tips and engaging stories.

For more information and free downloads, please visit Richard's blog site. If you would like Richard to speak at your event please contact him directly.

RICHARD CAN BE CONTACTED VIA:

Blog site:	www.richardmaun.com
LinkedIn:	Richard Maun
Twitter:	@RichardMaun
Business:	www.primarypeople.co.uk

plausible professional exterior – is it lion? Elephant? Crocodile? Or even meerkat? – you'll be better equipped to escape unscathed from your next brush with the boss. That way, you can make sure that you don't inflict on others the miseries you've had inflicted on you.

This book offers a lifeline for anyone suffering from a hostile work environment, and can help you transform the way you communicate and interact with others. It also contains a useful Personal Survival Kit, designed to help you really think about where you are and then take positive steps towards a happier, brighter and B@$T@*D-free future.

HOW TO KEEP
YOUR JOB

Brilliant ways to increase
performance, stay employed and
keep the money rolling in

RICHARD MAUN

Marshall Cavendish
Business

Published in 2011 by Marshall Cavendish Business
An imprint of Marshall Cavendish International

PO Box 65829
London EC1P 1NY
United Kingdom

and

1 New Industrial Road, Singapore 536196
genrefsales@marshallcavendish.com
www.marshallcavendish.com/genref

Other Marshall Cavendish offices: Marshall Cavendish International (Asia) Private Limited,
1 New Industrial Road, Singapore 536196 • Marshall Cavendish Corporation, 99 White Plains
Road, Tarrytown, NY 10591 • Marshall Cavendish International (Thailand) Co Ltd. 253 Asoke,
12th Flr, Sukhumvit 21 Road, Klongtoey Nua, Wattana, Bangkok 10110, Thailand • Marshall
Cavendish (Malaysia) Sdn Bhd, Times Subang, Lot 46, Subang Hi-Tech Industrial Park, Batu
Tiga, 40000 Shah Alam, Selangor Darul Ehsan, Malaysia

Marshall Cavendish is a trademark of Times Publishing Limited

A CIP record for this book is available from the British Library

ISBN 978 981 4346 28 3

Printed and bound in Great Britain by TJ International Limited, Padstow, Cornwall

For George and William

You both sparkle with talent.

Enjoy your successes and always keep learning.

CONTENTS

Preface

How To Keep Your Job is full of brilliant ways to improve performance, stay employed and keep the money rolling in. Probably the most useful book for anyone at work today, not least because it's based on real life examples of people who learned how to keep their job. Its central message is one of hope for us all — that we can assert ourselves and become an *Added Value Employee* — a respected and appreciated person within our organisation.

Are you facing cut backs or 'downsizing' issues at work and want to know how to reduce the chances of losing your job? Are you new into the world of employment and want to know how to survive? Have you taken months to find a job and wish to keep it? Are you under-performing or tired, or fed up with constant change and want to know how to turn things round? If you are, then you're not alone, but did you realise just how much you *can* influence the result — so that when the bosses decide who to keep and who to lose, you'll end up being one of the 'keepers' whom they hang on to?

You have more power than you realise and this book is here to help you unlock it, because it is possible to deploy strategies that will enable you to keep your job when others lose theirs. It is possible to turn round what may seem like a hopeless situation and it's possible to create goodwill and allow people to see your strengths in a positive light.

You can read this book and put the skills and strategies into effect and *really* be ahead of the curve. You'll know then you're somebody worth hanging on to – a high-performing *Added Value Employee*.

We are all good people who can have a successful and fulfilling working life. The trick is to know what to do to achieve this, which requires knowledge, insight and awareness. We need to know about the skills and the tools required for successful continuous employment. We need insight into how organisations work and we need awareness about our own behaviour, so that we can minimise the amount of time we spend irritating other people and maximise the amount of time we spend delighting them.

We also have to keep one thing in mind about our working life – which can slip from our grasp the second we walk through the door and begin our working day – that we are being *paid* for our services.

We are economic machines who need to provide a return on the money invested in us. Though this may sound cold and uncaring, it is the reality of our modern working world. We're not employed to keep the chairs warm and we're not employed for our good looks and charm, unless you happen to be a supermodel. We're employed because the organisation needs our skills and talents and is willing to pay for them. Real money changes hands and real time and resources are used up as we go about our work. Given that time, once spent, can never be recovered, we have to make good use of it in order to justify the money that is handed to us in return for our efforts.

This awareness of the economic contract that underpins our work is at the heart of this book. We have to remember it and make sure that we do everything we can to remain a high-performing individual, who is seen as a consistent producer of high quality output.

IT'S OUR LIFE

This book is here to provide practical guidance so that we can be really successful in our working life. However, we need to acknowledge that there are hundreds of possible careers and thousands of ways of interacting successfully with people. There are also notable examples of people who 'broke the rules' and things turned out well for them. These adventurous souls make for lively comparisons in cafés and at dinner parties, as people are often drawn to the cheeky renegade, the anti-hero or the person who rebelled and beat the system.

However, given the *millions* of people who go to work each day, these celebrated few are just that, a celebrated few. They will probably be successful in whatever they choose to do and however they choose to do it. That's great for them, but we have to recognise that until we can find our own style and the confidence to go our own way, we need to be good at keeping our job. If we're not, then we could be setting ourselves up for a miserable life and nobody deserves that.

Use this book to help you and at the same time remember that it's your life and you can choose how to live it. You decide what behaviour to exhibit, how to interact with others and to what standard you do your work. The responsibility for success, or failure, rests squarely on your shoulders. This book is here to support you, make things easier for you and fill in some of the gaps that we all have. I invite you to read it and to choose the bits that work for you. *Any* step forward that you take is one step away from failure and one step *towards success*.

BACKGROUND

This is a practical book, based on my real life experiences of working with people to help them keep their job. When working as an executive coach, I combine organisational awareness, process thinking and models of behaviour to provide clients with the insight and skills they need to increase their performance. Often, I'm hired to save people from exiting the organisation because with this unique combination of tools and models, I know what levers to pull and how to support people so that they regain their confidence and really excel at their work. In addition, I also lecture at a leading UK university, where I'm a visiting fellow, and run workshops for clients to enable people to develop their career skills.

I've also personally experienced the joy of being hired and the pain of having my job made redundant.[1] This even happened by email once, which has to be one of the most mean-spirited and callous ways of terminating someone's employment. So, I know what it's like to have to call your partner at 9.30am and break the news that you will be coming home early that day: to lick your wounds and wonder what went wrong. I've hired people and then had to let them go when their productivity failed to live up to the assertions they made at interview, and I've been involved in redundancy situations where I had to find ways of choosing between people. This is a stressful task, when you know that someone is going to lose their job and has a family to feed. I learned

---

[1] *We* are never made redundant. It's our *role* that is made redundant.

first hand that even though we work hard to make our criteria fair and reasonable there are still areas of subjectivity, because it's very difficult to make all such processes 100% objective.

Therefore, this book features real life stories and anecdotes and looks at what has worked to enable people to keep their jobs and to thrive within an organisation. In many cases the opening situations appeared hopeless, at least to the managers who hired me to work with their colleagues. To me though, there is always hope. People have vast reserves of skill and talent, and with some encouragement and support, these can be tapped and new ways of working can be instilled that break old destructive habits and lay the foundation for new and productive patterns of behaviour.

You can read this book and know that the content has made a real difference to people, who went on to make significant improvements to their working lives. They worked hard, learned new skills and kept their jobs. They became *Added Value Employees* and their lives went from stress and concern to those of celebration and longer term success.

You can be successful too – it's your life and the book is here to help you make it a great one.

ACKNOWLEDGEMENTS

Turning a book from an idea into a reality is a team effort and I would like to take a moment to acknowledge the people who have contributed to the success of this project.

Firstly, all my corporate clients, colleagues and delegates with whom I've worked deserve a big thank you. Thank you for your energy and for enabling me to learn with you – it's great to see people grow and develop.

Secondly, a warm and gracious thank you to Steve Tracey – who is great with feedback and has a knack of saying the right thing at the right time – for helping me to focus my thoughts and sharpen up the text. Thanks also go to Frances Donnelly, my faithful sounding board, who listens to my ideas and tells me straight if they need more work.

Thirdly, the good people at Marshall Cavendish need to take a bow and bask in my thanks and good wishes for all their hard work. Thank you particularly to Martin Liu for publishing this book and for all your support and encouragement. Also big thanks go to the design and editing teams, who provided good advice and who have worked patiently through the production process.

Although writing can be a solitary experience, there are a bunch of people who have kept me supplied with energy and smiles and whom I would have to invent if they didn't exist: Joe Holmes, Ria Varnom, Sarah Daniels, Steve Tracey again (he's that good), Debbie Robinson and Colin Brett; my office colleagues Paul O'Malley and Simon Hall, who generously allowed me to make tea and kept me amused with their witty banter; my ever-helpful friend Sara Greenfield who diligently followed up my emails so that I could find more time to write; and my special York Twitter-gang of Lindsay King, Julie Hewitt, Kathryn Todd, Heidi Forrest, Colin Merritt and Julie Holmes, who kept me company at odd hours of the day and night and offered encouragement and support when I needed it.

To all of you I say thank you again. You're all great and you're all part of the success of this book.

Right at the end there is a quiet space to say a wistful thank you to Keith Maun and Eric Ashby, both of whom are no longer with us. Both of you gave me positive role models for life and have made a big difference. Thank you for that and I know you're looking down and smiling as I write this.

And before we plunge into the heady cocktail of highly useful skills and tools that will help us to keep our job, there is one group of people who need hugs and kisses and bags of sugary sweets as a reward for being brilliant – so step up and take a bow my four noisy, boisterous and loving children: Lucy, Theodore, Oscar and Harvey. And lastly my deepest thanks are reserved for my supportive and loving wife, the talented and creative Beck. Thank you. Thank you all; you're the real stars here.

Richard Maun
England

RICHARD CAN BE CONTACTED VIA:

Blog site:	www.richardmaun.com
LinkedIn:	Richard Maun
Twitter:	@RichardMaun
Business:	www.primarypeople.co.uk

How It All Started

– Peter –

A TRUE STORY

It was one of those dull, slate-grey February days when it all went wrong. I parked my car and splashed through the cold puddles into reception, expecting to meet my client, a middle manager in a large, greasy factory full of high-speed printing machines. Instead I was greeted by a nervous-looking personal assistant, who said:

'Hello Richard, good to see you again. Instead of going straight into Peter's office, could you come with me please – Nigel wants to see you first, for a confidential *discussion*.'

Nigel was the fearsome managing director of the business and the PA's pronunciation of the word *discussion* made it sound like she was really saying 'confidential *shooting*'.

'Er, okay then,' I replied nervously, 'but I would prefer Peter to be with us. He is my client after all.'

'No, that's not possible right now,' she said, fixing me with a look, 'Nigel was most insistent that he speaks with you *first*.'

My stomach tightened and I wondered what was going on. I made my way up to Nigel's office, with a sinking feeling that suggested I wasn't going to a celebration and wasn't being invited up to the boardroom for tea and cakes! What had Peter done? What had I done? We would find out presently.

The meeting was brutally short. It went like this:

Nigel: Hello Richard. We have a problem.

Me: Hello Nigel. How's business? What's wrong?

Nigel: Business is tough and I need to sack Peter.

Me: (Speechless, gaping in shock.)

Nigel: But I don't want to sack him yet and I don't want him to know that I intend to get rid of him either.

Me: But but... he needs to know how you feel.

Nigel: No. His productivity is terrible and his confidence is worse. If you tell him about this it could destroy what little confidence he has left and then he will certainly have to go. I'm giving you a month to turn him round, or he's out.

Me: Can I have longer than a month? Six to eight weeks would be more reasonable.

Nigel: No. If he doesn't do something significant in the next four weeks he's out of here. Now I have to go to another meeting. Goodbye.

Me: Er, bye then.

Now, that was an interesting experience. I remember it vividly. At the time I already knew that Nigel had a reputation as a bully and that his leadership style could, at best, be described as unfriendly, and at worst, savage. I also knew that Peter had been contracted as a consultant and hadn't passed his probationary period and so could easily be removed.

I met with Peter and suggested we review his track record of achievements, which was fairly sparse. He knew he was struggling and was clearly nervous about getting the sack, even though we both knew he'd been working hard. He had failed to make an impact so far for some sound organisational reasons.[2] I then suggested that if *I* was his manager I *might* be thinking about removing him for such lacklustre productivity. After a few minutes of verbal jostling he took the hint and went white at the thought of losing his position.

'You can make it,' I reassured him, 'You just have to dig deep and change a few things, then I'm sure you will do well and be a success here.'

He looked doubtful, but said he'd try anything if it made a difference.

We worked together closely over the next four weeks and at the end of it I had a telephone call from Nigel saying how pleased he was with Peter's progress and that he was keeping him. Six months later, when Peter's contract came up for renewal, Nigel was all smiles as he offered him a permanent position. He was thunderstruck, however, when Peter resigned and informed him, with a broad smile, that he was leaving for a much better job in the factory on the other side of town. Not only had Peter kept his job and worked to the end of his contract, he had also learned how to work successfully in the business.

He had become an *Added Value Employee* and was now in the position to remain with the organisation, if he had wanted to do so. In his case he chose to move on, which would have been more difficult before, given his low performance. Success brings success and you're free to decide what to do with it.

---

[2] Including the fact that Nigel had deliberately withheld an agreed pay rise from the shop floor staff for three months just to prove he was the boss. Small wonder they didn't want to support Peter in making any changes then.

This book draws on the work Peter and I did to make a difference to him and it includes examples and stories from many other clients.[3] What they all show is that with knowledge and application, you can move yourself away from the exit and back into the organisation. When the others around you are fretting about their jobs, you can be reassured by the knowledge that there are many reasons for you to think positively because you've not been trusting to luck or burying your head in the sand. Instead, you've been working diligently to become an *Added Value Employee* – you have learned *How To Keep Your Job*.

As you read this book, you will learn some of the brilliant ways to improve your performance that have been used by people to make a significant difference to their working life. Each one is relatively simple and in combination they are hugely powerful. They include:

The AVE Concept Pg 30	4 Options for Change Pg 57	Contracting Questions Pg 94	20 Essential Communication Skills Pg 115
Organisational Impact Score Pg 40	10+ Ways to Increase Your Energy Pg 73	3Rs of Productivity Pg 98	3-Word Strap Line Pg 133
Keepers Cruisers Cutters Pg 43	The Dashboard Pg 82	4-Hour Lists Pg 100	The Metropolitan Model Pg 134
The Value Question Pg 54	7-Step Contracting Process Pg 90	Productivity Permissions Pg 109	Behavioural Anchors Pg 153

[3] Names and details have been changed to preserve client confidentiality.

Powerful You

– Take responsibility –

YOU HAVE MORE POWER THAN YOU REALISE

Power is the capacity to act proactively to make a difference. You have loads of it. That's the underlying message of this book. You have more power than you realise to shape your own future and it's up to you to take your power and use it. I've worked with people who were floundering at work and have managed to turn them round from nervous wreck to high performer. From being under the threat of expulsion to keeping their job and getting promoted. From being stressed and anxious to being calm and productive. I know what it's like to lose a job and how hard you have to work to find another one. I also know that most people trust to luck in order to keep theirs. In a competitive society, trusting to luck is no longer an option for long term employment success and it's vital that we acknowledge this and take positive steps to reduce our stress, increase our productivity and keep our jobs. It's no less than we deserve for ourselves and for our families.

We all have the power to influence our surroundings and

although there are times when we feel like a tiny part of an enormous resource-chomping machine, we *still* have power. This book is all about helping people to unlock that power and offering them practical suggestions so that they can wield it and make a difference. Whether you are a first jobber, a graduate on an internship, a successful manager with worries, or a hardworking individual who is deeply concerned about losing their job, this book is for you.

It often takes between 6 to 18 months to find a new job, so it makes sense to invest time and energy in keeping the one we have. This also reduces our stress and helps us to build a more satisfying working life and a happier and more stable home life.

Right now you might feel demoralised, or nervous, or maybe even laugh at the thought you can make a difference, but that thinking isn't helpful and you need to let go of it. Today you're going to read this book and realise just how resourceful you can be, and tomorrow you can start to put it into practice. Or you can start today if you want to – do something to signal the new you and your new approach to being successful.

THEY CHOSE US

You were chosen to join your organisation and you can be chosen to leave it. People make positive choices when they hire people and they make positive choices when they get rid of people. Although some businesses go bust and everybody loses their job, these are relatively rare within the general working population – the chances are that your organisation will at some point either introduce a new corporate strategy, or downsize, or use expansion as a way of sifting and sorting its employees. The ones they like will stay and the ones they don't will go.

Even if a whole office group or factory site is closed, the 'good people' will often be offered relocation packages, or sideways moves, or will be found a home in some part of the business. Senior managers are generally smart (although there are few dullards who make it based on their surname, or the old-boy-network) and they know that good people are hard to find, and that it makes sense to keep such people. Really good people are like gold dust and you *really* need to hang on to those.

Our task is a simple one: it's to take our power and get ourselves into a position where we become one of the 'keepers' – so that when a decision has to be made, and you can guarantee that one *will* be made at some time in the future – we fall into the band of people that the organisation will work hard to keep. This is because we will already have worked hard to become and remain someone whom the senior managers know and respect as an *Added Value Employee*.

THE *ADDED VALUE EMPLOYEE*

This book is about becoming an *Added Value Employee* – the goal that will help us to keep our job because, if we add value to the organisation, we increase our chances of keeping our place in it. If we add value to teams, we increase the chances that people will want to keep us in them and if we are generally well liked and well respected, then the organisation as a whole will want to keep us inside it.

We will measure our success at becoming an *Added Value Employee* throughout this book by referring to our AVE scores. The better we are, the higher our AVE scores will be and the more likely we will be to remain employed when everyone is sorted and compared on a value line from low scorers to high scorers. We want to be above the cut and with at least 20% of clear water in hand for an added safety margin. This means that we don't just want to be *good*, we want to be *great* so that when people are in discussion about what to do with us, a very short conversation will ensue, which will run like this:

'We need to decide what to do with Richard. We'll keep him. Put him on the pile over there and we'll sort him out later, after we've got rid of these people, whom, much as we "like" them, we can no longer afford to keep.'

An *Added Value Employee* has many qualities and attributes and we will consider how to develop these in this book. When we step back from details and boil them down to their essence, though, they fall into three main categories:

- Productivity
- People skills
- Public Relations (PR)

This is what I call the **AVE Concept** and we will explore it in greater detail in the next chapter. For now we need to recognise that scoring highly at *each one* of these things is essential, or we run the risk of losing our job. Our 'AVE scores' are the value we attach to our Productivity, our People Skills and our PR activities. Whatever your starting point is today, you have to remember that you *have more power than you realise* and that you have the skill and talent to succeed. If you're in doubt, go back and re-read the previous chapter and think about how Peter made the transition from plodding to performing. The secret to his success was to realise that he did have the power to make things happen, to negotiate with people and to make changes. His problem was essentially that he had forgotten that it existed within him.

THERE IS ALWAYS HOPE

When I'm coaching people, the first thing we do is to establish that there is *always* hope. That we can take positive actions to make a difference and that no matter how bad the situation seems, we *always* have options and we *always* have the capacity to act. We might only be able to take a tiny step, but it's still one pace closer to a brighter and more secure future and one pace away from disaster.

I've worked with some truly difficult cases, involving tears and tantrums and people who thought they were going to lose their job for sure, and yet we managed to turn things around to improve their situation. They moved from inactivity and worry to action and high productivity. I've included case studies and examples in this book so that you can read their stories and see for yourself that it's possible to make a difference in your working environment, to become an *Added Value Employee* and to significantly increase the chances of keeping your job.

DECISIONS INCLUDE EMOTIONS

One of the key reasons we know there is always hope is that people tend to make decisions based largely on emotional responses. People are always making choices. Whether to have salad or sandwiches for lunch. Whether to answer that email, or play another round of that game on their smartphone. Life is full of choices and two of the most important choices that are taken about us at work are:

- whether to employ us; and
- whether to keep us.

These *are* choices and although they are often dressed up in a legally pleasing jacket of facts and objective information, they are still choices which are made with imperfect information by flawed human beings. As a species we have one great defect when it comes to decision-making – most decisions are based on emotion.

People often amass facts and figures, check productivity charts and consult with complex ratios, but they also give in to their feelings. When we buy a house, we will consider how it feels to walk around inside it, whether we like the 'ambience' of the property and the view from the garden. When we buy a car or a piece of electrical equipment, we often include technical considerations in our thought process, but end up making choices with our hearts. Why else would products be styled and coloured to *look* appealing? If we were objective we'd buy the car that did the best job for us, but instead we buy the car because of the pretty headlights or the graceful sweep of the body lines, or the aggressive stance on the road, or because it looks cute and friendly.

We know we do this in our personal lives but we often forget that we do this in our professional lives too. So when the time comes for someone to make a choice about us, we can be sure that they will weigh up the 'facts' and then slap on a big dollop of emotion, to get the outcome they really want. If the wrong outcome occurs, then it's entirely possible to tweak the numbers and rerun the decision-making process to get the right answer. This allows them to defend their decision as being objective and open to scrutiny, which it is in part, but which is also laced with a healthy dose of emotion. The emotion is often held outside of our awareness and it is surprising just how often the people who leave an organisation are the ones who 'didn't fit in' and not the ones who 'fitted in, but did no work' or who 'didn't fit in, but had real talent'. Curious?

When people say that someone doesn't 'fit' their organisation, they are really saying that the behaviour deployed by that person isn't to the liking of that organisation. The concept of 'fit' is often used by people to excuse their own failings, but it's wrong to blame our departure on 'not fitting in' because every organisation encompasses a range of personalities who all seem to 'fit' in their own way. If we get the sack, we console ourselves by saying that we didn't fit in. What we should *really* be saying to ourselves is that we went because we didn't add enough value.

Instead of moaning and blaming other people or random events, we can keep our job by choosing to use behaviours that other people find helpful and rewarding to have around. One sad reality of 'fitting in' is that this is often used by bullying managers to describe junior staff who are subservient and don't give them any trouble – the kind of people who never challenge their authority and who never poke their own vulnerabilities.[4]

In other words, 'fitting in' is often an illusion and what counts is our *performance*. We need to know how many AVE points we have and what we need to do to increase our score, but before that, we need to make a choice to be successful.

WRITE A LIST OF POSITIVES

Part of choosing to be successful is about recognising that we have skill and talent, no matter what job we are doing, or how we currently feel about ourselves. Just because we may be stressed, doesn't mean that we have lost any of our goodness and one way to begin to see how good we might be is to write a list of our strengths

---

[4] If you work for a bully or know someone who does then have a look at the book **My Boss Is A B@$T@*D**. Despite the pithy title it's there to help people who are really stuck.

and skills. What do we do well? What have we had praise for in the last couple of years? What do we count among our achievements? What did they like about us at interview? What qualifications do we have (either on paper or through experience)? Take some time to think and perhaps chat with a trusted friend or your partner. Then fill in the table below, in any order, and feel free to add more items if you wish.

Strengths I have and achievements I have made include:	Technical skills and qualifications that I have include:
1)	1)
2)	2)
3)	3)
4)	4)
5)	5)

TAKING RESPONSIBILITY

We know that at some point in our working life, the organisation we are part of will expand, contract or maybe merge with a second organisation. At each one of these key decision points, the personnel required to make the organisation effective will change and therefore decisions will need to be taken about who stays, who goes, and who needs to be promoted or demoted. This is the time when things count, when our previous actions and inactions will be weighed up and decisions taken about us – when our AVE scores will be lined up and the people at the bottom weeded out. Our job is to ensure that our scores are high enough to survive the cut. It's as simple as that.

I'm inviting you here to acknowledge that you're a good person who works to the best of your ability and wants to do a great job. I'm also inviting you to acknowledge that there may be times when you under-perform, or have styles of communicating that annoy people. You might have been right to pursue your point and win the argument, but what was the cost in emotional terms? Are those people now waiting to get you?

Please go and fetch a pen and read the following statement, then sign and date it to give you a clear starting point in this book. In doing so you've made a positive choice to yourself and to your family. You're not going to be a passive worker who waits for the axe to fall. You're going to be the person you know you really are: talented, friendly, hard working and worth the money.

DECLARATION

I declare that I have chosen to become an
Added Value Employee.

I'm not going to sit idly by and worry. Instead I'm
going to gather information about what I do, reflect
on the changes I need to make and then make them
in order to increase my Productivity, my People Skills
and my PR activities. Though this may require an extra
effort, I believe that putting in this effort will be better
than having to find another job. I'm worth it and I'm a
good person – it's worth investing in me:

Signed:

Dated:

✳ SUMMARY

You have more power than you realise. You can choose to take your power and wield it effectively so that you increase your AVE scores, because the higher they are, the more likely you are to keep your job. You know that decisions always have a large emotional element and that if you have high AVE scores, people will tend to want to keep you. Even if they don't yet know what it is they want you to do exactly, they know that you're one of the 'keepers' who will be part of the organisation's future. Choose to become a 'keeper' and read on.

The AVE Concept

– The essence of success –

YOU CAN BE GREAT AT ALL THREE DISCIPLINES

Before we look at the AVE concept in more detail you need to know something which is a kind of secret that people in organisations often forget. The secret is that you are already amazing.

Think about how complex modern life is – we use sophisticated communications devices, we raise children; some of us act as school governors, or run sports clubs, or play a musical instrument. We negotiate and purchase property worth hundreds of thousands of pounds and drive cars which can travel huge distances and at great speeds. All of these things form part of our daily life and we overlook them because we just get on with it. However, if we look at the skills used to do these things we realise that they involve lots of thinking, lots of highly developed communication skills, the ability to embrace new technology and a constant updating of our transferable skills. Email, Twitter, Facebook, Skype, smartphones, blogging, digital cameras, video conferencing and online banking are all things that have become part of our daily lives. We've had to learn to use them and they all require the same skills that we need to be a successful *Added Value Employee*.

An example that I often use with clients, to make the point, relates to property and family: If I asked you to set up and manage a £1 million business you might shrink back and think, 'oh-my-god what a big scary project', and say, 'I could never do that. I'm not a business person, or a project manager.' However, if we look at 20 years of family income and include the value of property transactions, they can easily be in excess of £1 million. We manage that and we might even be doing a great job of it. There's no difference. If you can do it at home you can do it at work. And if you're struggling at home, you're probably just lacking a bit of support or information. I've worked with enough people who've moved from fed up, washed up and fearful to assertive, resourceful and productive to know that *we all have magic inside us*. We are talented and we can already do complex and demanding tasks.

Remember that, as you read this book, you're already doing it anyway. We just need to focus our thinking and actions to apply them to what we need to do in our organisation during our working day.

THE AVE CONCEPT

Building on the criteria of Productivity, People Skills and PR, we arrive at the AVE concept because it underpins what becoming an *Added Value Employee* is all about. The concept comes in two parts:

1   Scoring ourselves for each one of the three key areas.
2   Combining these raw scores into our Organisational Impact Score.

These will then show us where we need to improve and how much we contribute to the organisation overall. When we score highly, we become *Added Value Employees* and are more likely to keep our job. So this chapter is about how to work out our scores and then the rest of the book is devoted to practical changes that we can make in order to increase them. It's a very simple and very powerful process and it's worked successfully in many different organisations.

After extensive practical experience of working with clients I've come to see that in order to keep your job, all three key areas which we need to excel at in order to survive are *interlocking* for mutual support and success. Being good at only two of them isn't good enough as lacking the third could leave us vulnerable – much like building a castle and leaving one of the outer walls unfinished. We'd look impregnable from the front, but would be exposed to an attack from behind by marauding forces.[5]

AVE SCORES

Below is the AVE score table that we can use to work out how well we are doing in each of the areas. Please read the rest of this chapter and then come back and score yourself to give you a benchmark from which to gauge future performance increases.

---

[5] Several years ago I coached a client in a 'secure' factory. It had double-door locks on the front, a security buzzer, a camera and a secure waiting room. The back door, however, hadn't been wired into the alarm system and was frequently left hanging open. Don't make the same mistake when you're working hard to keep your job.

AVE SCORE TABLE	Do you do this rarely and/or badly?	Do you have good days and bad days?	Do you work to a consistently high standard?
	LOW AVE Score	MEDIUM AVE Score	HIGH AVE Score
PRODUCTIVITY	1 - 2 - 3 - 4	6 - 8 - 10 - 12	14 - 16 - 18 - 20
PEOPLE SKILLS	1 - 2 - 3 - 4	5 - 6 - 8 - 9	10 - 12 - 13 - 15
PUBLIC RELATIONS	1 - 2 - 3	4 - 5 - 7 - 8	9 - 10

The AVE concept invites us to think about what we do, because we need to imagine that we are being scored every day and, sadly, the reality of modern working life is that we're only as good as we were yesterday. The scales are deliberately weighted to reflect the fact that Productivity tends to carry more value than the other two factors and that an organisation will tend to tolerate someone who is a great performer and a bit grumpy, over someone who is a dazzling person to be with and yet constantly produces rubbish. People Skills are, however, vital and cannot be under-estimated. They go a long way to shaping people's opinion about us, particularly if we have to choose between two average performers – people will tend to back the one with better people skills and let go of the one with poorer people skills.

PR also has a bearing on our *Added Value Employee* status and comes third after the other two facets. If People Skills are about how you interact with your colleagues then PR is about who else knows you exist and knows you have skill and talent. People can score low on this scale and still keep their job, *but* I've noticed time and again that effective internal PR goes a long way to increasing our organisation's perception of just how valuable we are. Indeed many internal promotions arise because someone somewhere values our skills and talents and thinks we could do with a nudge to apply for the next role in our career.

Obviously other factors are likely to come into play when we think about what affects our organisational future and these might include corporate politics, tax changes, revised legislation, new consumer trends, or technological advances. However, those things are beyond our control, whereas our Productivity, People Skills and PR are ours to influence and improve.

As you read the rest of this book, reflect on your scores and perhaps refine them as you think more deeply about what you do well now and what you need to improve on. Set yourself a personal target to reach after one month of improvement activity, then re-score yourself and notice how much you have improved.

HOW TO SCORE YOURSELF

There are two ways to score yourself. Please choose the method that works for you for each of the three categories, and then circle the relevant number on each of the three scales. The first way is to use your instincts and circle one number on each line that best represents what you did over the last two to six months, depending on how good your memory is. It's okay to score yourself highly and it's okay to give yourself a low score too; what we want is for it to be realistic, rather than overly modest or needlessly harsh. Let your mind wander and gather a sense of how you would genuinely rate yourself if you were sitting in front of a panel of experts and had to justify how you arrived at those scores.

The second way to score yourself is to read the descriptors

below and then to decide which ones most closely fit you. It's likely that none of them will be a perfect fit, so use your judgement to decide which ones sound *closest* to your daily activities. Each one of the three disciplines is explained in more detail in the chapters that follow and when you reach them you can review your scores, as you consider your performance and think more deeply about just how much of each element you *really* put into practice.

PRODUCTIVITY is about delivering the right quality of work *on time*, every time. We're only as good as our last piece of work because people have short memories and tend to focus on the 'here and now'. Doing well two years ago and then doing nothing since isn't going to help.

✓ **LOW productivity** is characterised by work that needs constant supervision by others in order to correct mistakes, by work that is rushed and badly thought through and by missed deadlines. Missing deadlines always causes inconvenience to others and sends ripples through our local working environment. We might do some or all of these things for a majority of the time and recognise that this is a weakness we have, however well motivated we might be.

✓ **MEDIUM productivity** is characterised by work which can be termed 'acceptable'. It answers the brief and is delivered on, or close to, the deadline and only contains a few mistakes. Some days, or with some tasks, we might excel and this is balanced out by the days when we perform at reduced productivity levels, or have tasks that constantly frustrate us. People who perform at the upper end of the medium category will often show initiative and can solve problems with a minimum of support.

✓ **HIGH productivity** is characterised by work which can

always be relied upon by others to be delivered on, or before, the deadline, to be finished to a high standard and to need no, or only cursory, supervision for quality. Really high performers have a reputation for excellence and are often given the choicest tasks and more challenging roles, because they can be relied on to perform consistently. They show great initiative in completing tasks and are proactive problem solvers, who can balance thinking with doing and are able to self-monitor their progress and review where they are and where they need to go. Because of these highly developed transferable skills, they are often asked to support the work of other colleagues and/or departments.

PEOPLE SKILLS are about how well you get on with other people. Being quiet and methodical is a strategy for survival, being noisy and toxic is not. Being polite and thoughtful helps, while being abrupt, waspish and sour doesn't.

✓ **LOW people skills** are characterised by people who have a reputation for being argumentative, rude, aggressive, rebellious and miserable. They tend to snap at people and are tolerated rather than liked. There may also be loner types who, although they are great people inside, find it difficult to socialise with others and can be mislabelled as awkward or grumpy when they're just shy.

✓ **MEDIUM people skills** are characterised by people who get on well with some people, but not everybody. They will tend to have several friends and also to have a small group of people they struggle to relate to. Depending on who they are communicating with, they may be happy, laughing, warm, caring, polite, or abrupt, grumpy, teasing, gossipy, patronising or belittling. They may also flip from being serious to being humorous, which confuses people. They tend to forget that people don't like to be hurt and assume that as long as they have a few mates they'll be fine.

✓ **HIGH people skills** are characterised by people who are adept at mixing with all levels in an organisation. They ask purposeful questions *and* listen to the answers. They know how to sell ideas and how to overcome resistance. They are not passive or meek, but they know when to pursue a point and when to withdraw and put the relationship ahead of intellectual victory. They use language skilfully as a tool to get the job done and are comfortable presenting to groups. They are generally well liked, have few enemies and are considered to be polished performers within the organisation.

PR is the third key factor in our work to become an *Added Value Employee*. Public relations encompasses how the whole organisation perceives you and what you do to promote yourself and foster strong relationships around the *whole* environment. With good PR, people become aware of your skill set, your transferable skills and the potential you have to offer the organisation. If you think about yourself as a business then PR is about branding and differentiation[6] – your shop window. What special skills are you *known* for? How would you summarise yourself in 3 or 4 words? Why were you hired in the first place? Do you have a senior management mentor? Do you take part in discussion groups and clubs? Throughout the decision-making layer of the organisation, who knows you exist and who are your supporters? When a decision is made, people are often canvassed for their opinion and there are three broad categories that we all fall into:

1. Never knew him and never will. *We are asked to leave.*
2. Know him and don't like him. *We are asked to leave.*

---

[6] Differentiation means making people aware of what makes us special and unique in a positive way.

3. Know him and like him and think he's an asset. *Sometimes called 'a keeper'. We get to stay.*

✓ **LOW PR** scores are characterised by someone who is only known within their immediate team or work group, who has a poor relationship with their line manager and who tends to socialise only rarely, often at fixed functions, such as at a Christmas party. This may be down to a lack of knowledge – or a lack of confidence about how to become known – but it still rates as poor performance when we're considering AVE status. Low PR can also come about by the scoring of an 'own goal' in a significant situation, *i.e.*, making a mess of things in front of important people.[7]

✓ **MEDIUM PR** scores are characterised by people who have a reasonable working relationship with their line manager and who know at least one other manager who thinks well of them. They might also take part in a work-related activity such as a sports club, or socialise with people from outside their work group off-site. They don't actively seek out new opportunities to promote themselves, but are willing to take on new tasks and work with other departments and other managers when asked to.

✓ **HIGH PR** scores are characterised by someone who is known to a majority of managers and several directors, who all know what the person's key skills and talents are. High PR means actively networking within the organisation to make new friends and to come to the attention of the decision makers.

[7] As an example, I once asked the Directors of an organisation why they had purchased a particularly expensive piece of equipment. None of them could answer my apparently innocent question and collectively they all looked stupid. The problem was, of course, they all then disliked me for asking them that question, which had embarrassed them in a public setting. I know this because a colleague, who was in the meeting with me, reported back on their frowns and glares. Oops… a PR disaster!

This might be achieved by volunteering to take part in special tasks, or taking on occasional extra responsibilities, or by having a senior director as a personal mentor. High PR scores are about being effective in getting known as an asset, not about insincere friendliness or hard selling – these tend to irritate people. High PR scores also tend to go hand in hand with high productivity and high people skills, because it's pointless going out of your way to share major flaws with the senior management team – success brings success.

Now that you've read the descriptors, please go back and circle one of the numbers in the AVE score table for each category. Use your judgement and be honest with yourself. Perhaps discuss them with your partner as a safe way to check your thinking, or re-read your last annual appraisal. Choose a number for each category and choose now.

NATURAL VARIATION

Choosing a precise number can feel a bit self-limiting. If this applies to you, then we can recognise that although a best guess is still valid, we can think of a range of +/– 1 place on the scale for 80% of the time, to get an idea of where our true score is likely to be contained on most days. We can also think of a range of +/– 2 places for 20% of the time when we're either really flagging, or over-performing. (Note we're talking *places* here not points, because the scales are not all simple 1-2-3 progressions). So, for example, if you've scored yourself a 14 for productivity, that probably means some days you'll be a 12 and at the top end of the Medium category and on other days you might be a 16 and really producing excellent work. It's unlikely that you will dip into poor productivity, unless you're physically ill, or stressed, or have been asked to do a task for which you have no ability or training.

Keep this natural variation in mind when thinking about the Organisational Impact Score, because our true impact will tend to gently fluctuate within a range of scores. The key thing is to recognise what the general patterns are for you and not to get stuck arguing whether you should be an 8 or a 9 on one of the scales.

ORGANISATIONAL IMPACT SCORE

Now that we have our raw AVE numbers we can turn them into something useful to gauge how good we really are. Because these things all work in relation to one another we will *multiply* them together, in order to get an overall score that we can use to compare against other people. This is easier than it sounds even if maths isn't your natural strength, and we can work out our Organisational Impact Score by following the simple sum below:

> **My Organisational Impact Score is:**
>
> Productivity score of _____ x People Skills score of _____
>
> x PR score of _____ = _____
>
> All divided by 3,000 = _____

The number 3,000 is a constant and never varies and it reflects the maximum scores available for each category. If we multiply 20 x 15 x 10 we get to 3,000.

EXAMPLE: JACK AND HOLLY

Jack's work is adequate, he seems popular with his colleagues and is friendly with a couple of senior managers, with whom he plays football, so he scores himself 10 for productivity, 8 for people skills and 7 for PR. His scores look like this:

Jack's Organisational Impact Score
10 x 8 x 7 = 560 divided by 3,000 = 0.187

Holly works diligently and accurately, can be grumpy if disturbed while she's working and tends not to socialise too much with her colleagues, so she scores herself as 16 for productivity, 4 for people skills and 1 for PR. Her scores look like this:

Holly's Organisational Impact Score
16 x 4 x 1 = 64 divided by 3,000 = 0.021

In comparing Jack and Holly's Organisational Impact Scores we can see that although Holly is more productive, the effect of multiplying scores makes a big difference to her overall score. It's more likely that in this case the organisation will choose to keep Jack because his work isn't significantly worse, but his people skills and his PR skills are significantly better. Although working life requires us to be productive, it is also a social environment and people like to feel good about their colleagues and enjoy their company.

WHAT IS A GOOD SCORE?

Our aim is to be as close to 1.000 as possible, as that is the maximum score. In the examples above, neither Jack nor Holly scored particularly well because this system highlights the problems of being average for most things, or great at one thing and poor at the others. It also means that a small improvement in one area can have a great impact. If we imagine that Holly read this book to the end, chose to put some of the things into practice and that her people skills and PR scores increased by several points each, then her updated Organisational Impact Score might look like this:

> **Holly's New Organisational Impact Score**
> 16 x 8 x 4 = 512 divided by 3,000 = 0.171

By putting in extra effort to improve the way she interacts with her colleagues and by doing some basic networking, perhaps to remind people that she can be a fun person and just likes to work undisturbed, Holly's Organisational Impact Score has increased from a tiny 0.021 to a more respectable 0.171. This means that in practice she's around the same level as Jack, and if the organisation really values her productivity then she will be the one to be kept, if they had to make a choice.

That's one of the key things to remember; whilst poor effort multiplied together gives a really low OI score, small improvements can have *huge* effects – that's why there is *always* hope. You don't often have to do much more work to become an *Added Value Employee* and increase your chances of keeping your job.

AVE CLASSIFICATION AND
ORGANISATIONAL IMPACT SCORE ZONE

As an Organisational Impact Score in isolation can be a bit meaningless, we can use the following table to give ourselves a sense of perspective and find out how close we are to becoming an *Added Value Employee*. The example scores are just indicators – the key thing to focus on in the table is where your Organisational Impact Score sits and to note the *zone* this tends to place you in and what *type* of employee this might describe you as:

TYPE	Example Productivity Score	Example People Skills Score	Example Public Relations Score	OI Score	ZONE
KEEPERS	20	15	10	Max 1.000	**SAFE** This is the best zone to be in and where we all need to aim for. We need to score at **least 0.420** to be here. When we're here then we really are *Added Value Employees*
	14	10	9	0.420	

CRUISERS	12	9	8	0.288	**STRESS** This is where the majority of people sit and the danger here is that we could end up close to the 'cut'. We need to score at least 0.040 to be here.
	6	5	4	0.040	
CUTTERS	4	4	3	0.016	**SO LONG** This is the worst zone to be in and there is a high chance of leaving the organisation if we stay here.
	1	1	1	0.001 Min	

The table shows combinations of scores for each classification and it's possible to be in the *Safe* zone by excelling at productivity and people skills whilst being average at PR. This is because organisational PR performance tends to lag behind Productivity and People Skills in real life. However, it's not possible to get into the *Safe* zone if we're poor at PR and great at the other two, which serves to remind us that it's the *combination* that counts. It also tends to suggest that for many people an improvement in PR will accelerate them higher up the *Cruiser* group and away from the majority of their colleagues.

The effect of multiplying scores is that we need to achieve a *minimum* Organisational Impact Score to enter each area. Anything below **0.040** and we're in the *Cutter* group, whatever our combination of AVE scores are which make this up. Similarly, if our combination of AVE scores put our Organisational Impact Score at **0.420** or above then we can relax a bit, knowing that we've joined the elite group of *Keepers* and can think of ourselves as high-performing *Added Value Employees.*

If we're in the *Safe* zone then there is a high chance the organisation will keep hold of us, as we will tend to have useful transferable skills and be considered an asset. The *Stress* zone is so named because people in it face the most uncertainty in terms of keeping or losing their job. Clearly there is a hierarchy here, based on Organisational Impact Scores, but as we won't know where the cut line is we cannot allow ourselves to be complacent. We need to keep on improving because even a modest increase will reflect in a much higher Organisational Impact Score. Finally, if our productivity is generally dreadful then we can expect to be in the *So Long* zone, because that's what we're likely to hear fairly soon from our line manager… *so long buddy… there's the door… please use it… goodbye!*

Some enlightened employers will recognise that if someone is in the *So Long* zone they need help and support. People tend not to hire poor performers and then pay them for doing very little, so if someone is here then it's likely that something is amiss and ought to be investigated. Perhaps the person concerned has problems at home, has a health issue they're not sharing, or has been over-promoted and is struggling to keep up in a new role. Huge organisational changes can sap people's confidence and energy and in times of uncertainty it's likely that some people, when they most need to shine, find it hard to cope and end up struggling. If you know someone who is struggling, find a way to help them because we all need a little support sometimes.

To get a really high Organisational Impact Score we need to be consistently good in all three categories. However, don't be disappointed if your score seems low; that's the effect of multiplying things together and then dividing them. They produce small numbers at the end. However, if we make a small change in our basic AVE Score it can have a big impact. Equally, if we're superb at one area, such as Productivity, but are lousy at something else, such as People Skills, then our Organisational Impact Score will be dragged down and rightly so. Use the rest of this book to help you increase your scores, reduce your stress and improve the pleasure of your daily work experience. Success brings success and a great sense of comfort, so it's worth making a little extra effort to reap great rewards.

✻ SUMMARY

Our Organisational Impact Score is the jumping off point for making improvements. It gives us a sense of where we stand in the organisation and what we have to do to get into the elite *Safe* zone where the high-performing *Keepers* live. If we're already there we can still find ways to increase our performance because scores will tend to fluctuate over time and even the greatest people can have bad days, or a run of poor productivity.

To be successful *Added Value Employees*, we need to recognise that there are three basic underlying areas of our work: our Productivity in terms of what we do and how we do it; our People Skills, in terms of how we fit in with the world around us and our PR activity in terms of how we become known and build our influence throughout the rest of the organisation. Remember too that perception counts because, no matter how objective and fact-based a selection process is, it often involves an element of emotion and therefore contains some personal bias; that's why we need to perform to a consistently high standard in all three areas. High performance is available to all of us; it's all about making sure we put simple tips and tools into practice.

The Value Question

– Living in an economic environment –

YOU CAN BE A VALUABLE ASSET TO YOUR ORGANISATION

Are you value for money? To keep your job you need to be. It's a *vital* principle which many people overlook at their peril. We need to be paid for our time so that we can buy food, look after our families and generally live a pleasant and comfortable life. This is a perfectly reasonable position and selling our time is what work is all about. However, we need to balance what we get paid with what we give back.

The value we place on our time is contingent on the skills and talents we use to fill it with, so someone performing life saving medical surgery tends to get paid more than someone wielding a broom to keep the streets tidy. Both jobs are important to society, but they have very different values attached to them. However, as the stress of looking for work fades away and people settle into their jobs, people can start to lose sight of the financial side of their working life. When we don't have a salary, we soon realise the value of money and yet, once we have been employed for a few months, we get comfortable with the fact that money is going into our bank on a regular basis. The transfers are often made electronically, so we don't see the money – it becomes an abstract concept. We pay for products with plastic cards – again no physical cash changes hands, so we lose our sense of cause and effect and it becomes something that happens, like breathing.

Breathing just happens. We get on with it without a second thought, unless we get a cold, or suffer from asthma, or hay fever. Then we value the ability to breathe clearly. Money is the same and what helps people to keep their job is by remaining sensitised to the reality that they're operating inside an *economic environment*.

So, accepting that we work for money, here's a question – what's the total cost of employing you? Pause for a moment and think about it.

YOU ARE A RACEHORSE

Horses are expensive pets and make for a costly hobby, so it's no surprise that, in the UK, horse racing is called 'The Sport of Kings'. In our working environment, we are like racehorses in that when we walk into an organisation we cost money to house and to look after. Whatever job we do, we're an expensive luxury that causes people to spend money that they'd rather not have to spend. I used to work with a finance director whose accurate mantra was:

'Overheads walk in on two legs.'

I thought this was a bit cynical until I realised that he was referring to the *consequences* of employing people in terms of the whole cost to the organisation. So, in that regard, we really are racehorses and need to think of ourselves as such – special, talented people who deserve to be well treated and who, in return, are worth our keep. Because if not, like racehorses, we will get 'retired'.

YOUR DIRECT COSTS

Direct costs are all the items that cause us to be paid money which, if we weren't there, could be saved or be put to other uses. They're more than our salary and often bigger than we realise. Have a look at the following table and add in a number for each category. It's fine to make an educated guess, rather than leaving a space blank. There's an example column to help you if you're not comfortable writing your own figures in.

DIRECT COSTS OF KEEPING YOU PER YEAR (THE MONEY WHICH GOES TO YOU)		
Basic Salary	£30,000 (example)	£
Overtime Payments	£ 3,000	£
Annual Bonus	£ 1,000	£
Pension Contributions (If not known, assume 5% of basic salary)	£ 1,500	£
Company Car Allowance (If not known, assume £5,000 pa)	£ nil	£
Other Rewards (Reward schemes, vouchers, etc)	£ nil	£
TOTAL	**£35,500**	**£**

YOUR INDIRECT COSTS[8]

These are all the ancillary costs that are picked up by the organisation as a result of us being there. While that's part of our working life, we still need to recognise that they exist because otherwise we could under-value the total cost of our employment, and that could lead us to reduce our efforts to add value. The more people an organisation employs, the more it needs to spend on management and administration to support the people delivering the service or making the products. As with direct costs, look at this table and add in your figures, taking an educated guess where reasonable. Again, there's an example column if you're not comfortable about writing in your own costs.

INDIRECT COSTS OF KEEPING YOU PER YEAR (THE ADDITIONAL MONEY WHICH THE ORGANISATION SPENDS ON YOU)		
Employer Tax and National Insurance (NI) Contributions (Assume 15% of your basic salary + overtime + bonus)	£ 5,100	£
Recruitment Costs (Assume it costs 2% of your salary per year to replace you)	£ 600	£
Annual Training Costs (Assume about £1,500 as an average, unless the true amount is known)	£ 1,500	£
Tools, software, licensing costs for software use, general desk/bench equipment (If not known assume £1,000 as a contribution to centrally purchased items)	£ 1,000	£

[8] The figures used in this chapter have been adapted from UK data sources, such as the Chartered Institute of Personnel & Development, the Confederation of British Industry and HM Government.

Telecomm Costs (Mobile phone fees, internet access, etc. If not known assume £200)	£ 200	£
Travel, subsistence and accommodation (Make a guess if not known)	£ nil	£
Office overheads – 2% of basic salary (Heat, light, ground rent, electricity, etc)	£ 600[9]	£
Management overheads – 5% of basic salary (The need to have a manager or supervisor above you, for example)	£ 1,500	£
Administration overheads – 5% of basic salary (The cost of running the payroll, and personnel functions on your behalf)	£ 1,500	£
Consumables (Drinks, paper, printer ink, toilet roll, washing up liquid, etc. If not known, assume £100)	£ 100	£
Others (Specialist training, or equipment such as safety boots that tends to be updated on a regular basis)	£ 50 safety boots And/or £ 2,000 for specialist laundering of work clothes	£
TOTAL	£12,150	£

GRAND TOTAL

Now please add the two numbers together to see how much it costs to keep you in the organisation and then be prepared for a surprise:

[9] You could argue that if you weren't at work this cost wouldn't really be saved, but it's possible to move a smaller number of staff to a smaller office or workshop. If you don't feel comfortable with this, then feel free to take it out.

COST OF KEEPING YOU		
Your Direct Costs (The money you receive)	£ 35,500	£
Your Indirect Costs (The additional money paid out by the organisation)	£ 12,150	£
TOTAL	**£47,650**	**£**

You will notice that the indirect costs in the example are one-third of your direct costs. While you might be surprised that this is much higher than you think, you're in for a shock – estimates have suggested that the *extra* costs of employing someone may be between 40% and 100% of their salary. This means that a person on a salary of £35,000 could cost their organisation up to £70,000 per year in total, which throws added focus on the need to be an *Added Value Employee*.

And you thought you weren't a racehorse?

HOW MUCH ARE YOU WORTH?

Now that we have a sense of our costs to the organisation we can think about the *Opportunity Cost*. Opportunity cost is a term that means the cost of doing an alternative thing. For example, if you could have earned £500, but decided to spend the same time earning £200 instead, then you have cost yourself £300. You had the opportunity to earn more, but your decision cost you £300, hence the term *Opportunity Cost*. In terms of keeping our job, we need to make sure that the organisation gets a great return on their investment and working out our total costs helps reinforce just how expensive we are to have around: if we cost our organisation £70,000 and are not returning enough value, they may decide to find out what else they could buy for £70,000 per year.

THE VALUE QUESTION

Now that we know how much we cost to the organisation, there is a question which we have to ask ourselves, when considering our costs *and* our *Added Value Employee* Scores *and* our *Organisational Impact Score*. This question is this:

How much would you pay for you?

If you had to put a financial value on your performance over the last six months, what would it be? Be honest here and if you've done well – perhaps landing a huge order if you're a sales person – then own up to your success. Also, if you know you're falling behind your targets, then acknowledge that too, because someone, somewhere, will have a spreadsheet with your numbers on it. Use this question as a way of cross-checking your Organisational Impact Score from the previous chapter. Do the two match up? Have you over-inflated your Organisational Impact Score in relation to your perceived value?

Whatever the outcome, we can use this information to reinforce our recognition that we work in an economic world and that, if people are being paid for under-performing, then their continued survival is under threat. Conversely, you may be a high earner and a high performer: then the organisation will have to balance the cost savings they can make by getting rid of you with the *risk* of losing the excellent return on their investment that you make for them.

EXAMPLE: ALBERT AND ISAAC

To see the effect of value in action, we can look at two managers, Albert and Isaac, who both worked for the same organisation. Albert was a line manager who did a passable job of keeping his team of 12 administrators working effectively. Although he didn't excel, he didn't make that many mistakes either. Then, one day, Isaac arrived to oversee the business and was full of energy and keen to make improvements. All went well and Isaac started to increase the department's performance. Then the organisation failed to win a key contract that it was bidding for, for a large piece of business in France, and now it needed to reassess its staffing needs and management structure. Realising that they could only afford one manager, the owners faced a choice. What should they do?

Although Isaac cost more to employ than Albert and the company could have saved more by getting rid of him, they knew he'd improved productivity and reduced the number of mistakes in customer orders. His Organisational Impact Score was higher than Albert's, who had recently been causing problems by stubbornly failing to complete reports on time. Also, Albert had been complaining bitterly about some of the changes Isaac was instituting. The owners decided to make Albert's job redundant and, as there was no other opportunity for him, he left the organisation still grumbling fiercely that he was clearly the cheaper manager and should have been the one to stay.

The owners had clearly weighed up both Organisational Impact Scores and perceived value in their decision-making process; their decision wasn't about saving the most money, but was about making sure they continued to get the most *value for money*.

✳ SUMMARY

We live and work in an economic environment and even if we're an intern on minimum or no wages, we still cost the organisation money in terms of the indirect costs that are attached to us. Nothing is ever free. Getting a true sense of our total cost to our organisation is useful information that keeps us aware of the need to return value to offset the money spent on us.

If we feel hopelessly stuck, then there *are* options to help us get moving and even if they involve a loss of face – or having to finance these options ourselves – that's always cheaper than losing our job. If you think hiring a coach is expensive, then imagine the opportunity cost to you of being out of work. It starts to make the former look like a cheap option. And if money is tight, we can talk to our friends – or perhaps trade skills with people – to get what we want. That has to be better than nothing and is certainly better than sitting in silence.

You can add value to your organisation and you can move yourself up to being a high performer who outweighs his costs of employment, by becoming an *Added Value Employee*. You can because you're worth it.

Practical Options

– We have more options than we realise –

YOU CAN MAKE CHANGES

If you recognise that you are overpaid and under-performing, it makes sense to discuss options with your line manager, or human resources department, and to be active in finding a solution. Many people wait until the axe falls and then mount a valiant defence of their potential contribution to the organisation. That rarely works because once an organisation has decided to live without you, they tend to stick with their decision. That is, unless you obviously fit into other roles, or have decided to lodge an appeal against unfair dismissal. Exercising your right of appeal is always worth considering and asking for a copy of the appeals procedure would be the first step to take.

In terms of making progress and being proactive, here are four classic options for change to bring your perceived value back into line with your Organisational Impact Scores. They include:

1. **Asking for further training**. This shows commitment and requires a financial investment, however small. It might give you the tools you need to do the job or some new found enthusiasm to increase your performance. You might

even offer to contribute some of the training costs out of your own pocket, or offer to make up the time lost due to training.

2. **Asking for coaching or mentoring.** I'm always astonished that an organisation will buy a machine, such as a printer-copier, and insist that it comes with a maintenance contract, and yet the same organisation will hire employees and park them at a desk, leaving them to get on with their tasks alone. Even if there is an induction period, it's often of the fire-and-forget type that pays no attention to how people really learn. If you think you're struggling, or are just a bit lost somehow, then getting professional external support is a smart move. Even if you have to pay part of the costs yourself, that's still cheaper than spending six to twelve months looking for work. I used the word *external* here deliberately; you want to work with someone whom you completely trust and who has no conflict of interest. It's rare to find these people within your organisation simply because everyone has a boss and an agenda of their own, however much they may say otherwise.

3. **Asking to keep your role and to move to a different team.** Sometimes changing personal dynamics can make a big difference. I managed an administrator once whose previous manager had loathed her, due to her perceived poor performance. I didn't know her, so when she came to work for me we started over afresh and she did really well. Same person, same job, different manager, different rapport. Result? Excellent performance.

4. **Asking for another role.** This may involve letting go of some responsibility and may feel like a small humiliation, but people often have really deep respect for those who know what their talents are and recognise their shortcomings. It's always better to be proactive and have a discussion, rather than plod on, waiting to be tapped on the shoulder and invited on a one-way trip to the personnel manager's office to receive a 'brown envelope'.[10]

---

[10] Tax forms and governmental instructions tend to come in brown envelopes; they signify that something important and generally unpleasant is inside – in this case usually our final wages and the terms of our severance.

EXAMPLE 1: KATHERINE

Katherine was an excellent personal assistant who could type quickly, was polite on the telephone, organised the team diary well and was generally relied upon by everyone. So, naturally, she was promoted to the role of office supervisor, for which she had no training and had no inclination or ambition for. She was a disaster almost from the start and found it harder to manage people directly than when she had to simply chase them up for diary dates. Her stress increased, her health dipped and her performance plummeted. The organisation decided she had to go and she was earmarked for redundancy at the earliest opportunity.

However, she was proactive and, realising that her role was under threat, she approached her line manager and asked that she be moved back to being a personal assistant. This involved a small pay cut and a much bigger loss of prestige, and her manager was astonished at her request. However, observing that she had 'lost a great PA and gained a poor supervisor', the manager agreed she could move back, as the personal assistant role hadn't been filled yet. Within a week her performance had soared back up and, despite a few teasing comments from her colleagues, she was happy again.

Katherine then survived a round of redundancies that saw many people leave the organisation, including a couple of particularly waspish colleagues who had teased her persistently and, in doing so, had failed to consider their own performance. Being wedded to a job title, a ritzy business card and a leather swivel chair is a sign that you're in deep trouble. Humility goes a long way, and displaying it is a really sensible thing to do.

EXAMPLE 2: STEVE

Steve was hired as a managing director for a service company that specialised in fixing building problems. Despite having been hired for his brusque no-nonsense style and asked to make changes, he was facing a mutinous backlash from his staff and managers, who found him cold and imposing. Recognising that he was overpaid and under-performing and yet (for the short term) replacing him would be costly, the organisation hired me to work with him. I soon found out that Steve had never been an MD before and had been given no direction or management training; he was well paid, but clueless. During our sessions, I enabled him to realise that, in his organisation, an MD was meant to manage the business *and* win new customers, and I worked with Steve to develop strategies and the confidence to achieve this. At our second meeting, Steve reported that he had visited his first customer, who was staggered that a busy managing director had found the time to come and see them. As a result of making a good impression and identifying an opportunity for new business, he left with a contract worth £100,000. After that, Steve never looked back. He calmed down his style, won more business, developed better relationships with his staff and designed and implemented a detailed improvement strategy. His improvement was so marked that, after two years, he was promoted to become a Global Vice President. The first thing he did after agreeing to this new challenge was to book more coaching to help him make a smooth transition.

Although Steve hadn't instigated the initial coaching for himself, he did recognise that getting support was a major factor in his success. So when a junior manager was struggling, he was quick to arrange coaching for her and she soon improved. We all tend to face increased stress when presented with a new challenge and being resourceful and getting support can make the difference between spectacular success and total failure. It's okay not to know all the answers and to have gaps in your skill set, or to need a confidence boost. Getting a professional coach to work alongside you, or developing a mentoring relationship with a trusted person, is the move of champions. Can you think of a successful sports person, or singer, or dancer, who did it all on his, or her, own? I can't; they all have coaches.

ACTIVITY COUNTS

If we want to keep our jobs we can't stay ignorant, or push things to one side and sort them out 'tomorrow'. That may be a day too late for us. We have to keep things in our awareness so that we can update our productivity, remain open to new opportunities and celebrate success. Remaining in awareness also makes us more likely to be *proactive* and, instead of chewing our way through our working day like a big bag of nerves, we *can* do something about it. However, remaining 'passive' means we are actively putting our energy into staying stuck. It takes energy to fret, to gossip and to keep ourselves tight shut and well defended. It makes more sense to realise this and invest the same energy into problem solving, because when we do that, the world suddenly becomes a much brighter and happier place.

✳ SUMMARY

The messages for us to take to heart are simple and clear:
1. We always have more *options* than we realise.
2. We can stop being passive and we can be *active*.
3. We can begin to *solve* our own performance issues.

The choice is ours. Act now. Make a commitment to change and do something positive. A happier future awaits us and we deserve it.

TKO Time

– Avoiding obvious mistakes –

YOU CAN BE SMART

Amazingly, many people lose their jobs because they make a fundamental mistake or fall foul of personnel procedures. These incidences tend to be called a TKO – a 'Technical Knock Out' – because your performance becomes irrelevant. You would be leaving however high your Organisational Impact Score is and, as we don't want that to happen, we need to learn from those unfortunate souls who have fallen foul of a TKO before.

Human resources procedures are designed to ensure fairness and clarity so that the organisation has clearly defined and published processes to follow and can legitimately manage its business. However, they can also be used to get rid of people because they also legitimise the reason for dismissal. In order to keep our job, we need to remember that there are a few things worth *not* doing. So, this chapter is about what *not* to do.

Pause for a moment and ask yourself how many ways are there to suffer a TKO? Can you think of more than ten? Here is a list of traps to watch out for and, although most of them are blindingly obvious, it's prudent to take them all seriously as people get tripped up by them all the time:

1. **Don't steal.** Stealing by staff is reputed to account for 51% of all thefts in shops. While some people might have their fingers in the petty cash, there are other ways to steal. For example, if you help yourself to a drink from shop stock because you're a thirsty shop assistant, that's actually stealing. Most thieves are caught when they go on holiday and a temp notices something is wrong, or during a formal audit where stock figures are reconciled with what is actually in the warehouse.

2. **Don't steal by accident.** This is where you get caught out by a technicality. A client of mine revealed that he had lost his job because he had 'falsified his expenses'. This sounds ghastly, given that several MPs have been charged with false accounting. In his case, however, what he had done was to claim the cost of a hotel room without a receipt, with the full knowledge of his boss. The payroll department spotted the error and he was dismissed. The fact that this coincided with a major restructure – and that other people had done the same thing and went unpunished – turned out to be good grounds for taking his employers to an industrial tribunal. He was unlucky, but he *had* broken the rules, even though it was a small breach.

3. **Don't break the law.** This can be a cause for dismissal and I know people who have lost their jobs because they were banned from driving. One for speeding and one for falling asleep at the wheel. If your job depends on a skill such as driving then it's really not worth drinking, speeding, texting or falsifying your tachograph. If you do, you'll have a long time to reflect upon it.

4. **Don't bring your company into disrepute.** If you break the law and your court case gets into the papers, you can be dismissed for causing bad PR to your organisation.

5. **Don't break iron rules.** These are where the organisation has
    clearly demarcated 'no-go' areas that lead to instant dismissal.
    An example of this would be delayed payment in a betting
    office. The teller has to take the cash at the point the bet
    is made. If she gives you unofficial credit on the promise
    that you'll 'pay her back tomorrow', she is liable for instant
    dismissal if found out – a manager I knew was fired for this.
    He was a decent manager and the organisation really liked
    him, but iron rules are not for bending. He had to go.

6. **Don't break health and safety rules.** If you have to wear
    safety shoes, you have to wear them. We had to stop
    production in a factory once because several machine
    guards had been removed and the supervisors were warned
    that a second case of infringement would lead to dismissal.
    There is never an excuse for poor health and safety practice.

7. **Don't lie on your CV.** The company can legitimately claim
    that you misrepresented yourself and that they may not
    have employed you had they known the truth.

8. **Don't lie on your application form.** This is the same as
    the above and if you're asked to fill one out, make sure it
    matches your CV. Many people are found out because the
    two don't match, or references are unable to substantiate
    their claims.

9. **Don't breach confidentiality.** Often hard to prove, but if
    it happens, prepare for the worst. A classic way to breach
    confidentiality can occur when a person is under notice of
    redundancy and makes a call to a supplier or competitor
    to vent their frustration. A senior manager I knew did this
    once and was found out when the competitor telephoned
    the managing director to find out if the news was true! His
    contracted was terminated about ten minutes later.

10. **Don't forget your work permit.** A colleague came to the
    UK from India to study and then to work and assumed he
    would get a work permit. He didn't. He had to leave or risk
    being deported. He was a good person too and we were sad
    to see him go, but go he did.

11. **Don't be discriminatory.** Race, sex, age, religion, disability. Take your pick. Newspaper comments about the world going politically correct are not a defence in law and if you think you have some problems with this, then seek help. We all have rights and we don't have to take rubbish. We don't deal it out to people either.

12. **Don't use the internet for looking at naked people.** I think the correct term is 'surfing for porn' and this can lead to a charge of gross misconduct, if found out. I visited a high-tech facility once that contained an embedded research unit, with highly restricted entry. After a routine survey of internet activity by the IT department, it was discovered that one of their senior researchers – thinking he was safe from prying eyes in the secure area – had been involved in a bit of 'freelance research' during working hours. He left the business soon afterwards.

13. **Don't exceed your authority.** Signing cheques that you aren't entitled to or authorising purchase orders which are above your signatory limits could be deemed as fraud. If you don't know your signatory limits, then find out what they are.

14. **Don't fall foul of substance abuse.** Companies are increasingly giving employees routine drug tests, particularly if they're in charge of machinery or involved in driving jobs. If you like to smoke cannabis, do you know how long it stays in your system? The consensus is that traces can remain in your body for between three days for light occasional usage and *up to 3 months* for prolonged and regular usage. That means waiting 90+ days to be really sure you're all clear. Also, beware of breath tests and checks on alcohol consumption; those extra pints in the pub at lunchtime could be disastrous.

15. **Don't make a catastrophic mistake.** This could be termed gross misconduct, especially if it's not your first offence. I once made a mistake on a purchase order and a lorry turned up with one roll of paper on it, instead of 16, making the customer's already late order even later and jeopardising

their continued business with us. Although I wasn't dismissed, I was kicked round the car park for the mistake. A second one would have been curtains though.

16. **Don't get sacked for listed gross misconduct offences.** These include fighting, horseplay and dangerous driving, such as with a fork-lift truck. Letting off fire extinguishers or using compressed air lines to clean off dust are also pretty dangerous. Your HR handbook will tend to list these offences, so you know what to look out for.

17. **Don't call your boss a 'bastard'.** A surprising entry perhaps, but I did this in one of my earliest jobs. The boss in question was, unknown to me, standing behind me at the time when I addressed my opinion to the whole office, just to make sure everyone knew how I felt. Although I apologised heartily, which he 'accepted', he also put me on the list for redundancy. In the end, I had a lucky escape and kept my job because I didn't actually work directly for him and was 'rescued' by the finance director who happened to be mentoring me and knowing that I actually worked for one his accountants promptly took me off the list.

18. **Don't get blind drunk at a party and goose the MD's wife.** This could be termed assault or, at the very least, an act of gross misconduct. Christmas parties are fraught with danger. A junior worker got very drunk at a Christmas party and started slinging abuse at one of the directors. He was dragged away by his deeply embarrassed wife and, although he didn't get dismissed for it, his 'card was marked' and he did leave the organisation soon afterwards. His PR score, had he been aware of it at that point, would have registered a disastrous *minus* 20!

MISCONDUCT MAY NOT BE GROSS

The term *gross misconduct* means that we have committed a major transgression and are liable for dismissal. However, not all offences fall into this category – some are termed simply as *misconduct*. The example above of accidental stealing could fall into this category because the organisation had a range of reasonable courses of action open to them, e.g. an initial warning, or an inquiry into what had happened, or even some kind of training to increase employee-awareness of procedures.

Just because an organisation has a handbook that lists things as gross misconduct, it doesn't always mean that they would be held up as such in a court of law, or in an industrial tribunal. If procedures are badly defined, arbitrary or genuinely hard to follow, there may be a case for discussion and review. However, it's not wise to be the person to put them to the test by losing your job and fighting for compensation!

DO THESE THINGS

Following the long list of *don'ts*, here are the key *do's* to focus our attention on something productive. Which ones do you need to pay particular attention to?

- ✓ Stop and think.
- ✓ Take a deep breath before you act.
- ✓ Count to ten when you feel yourself getting cross.
- ✓ Take a sip of water before speaking.
- ✓ Stick to procedures.
- ✓ Know the rules.
- ✓ Remember that the truth will tend to come out during an audit, or when you're on holiday.
- ✓ Ask people to supply a reference for you and tell them about the job you're going for.
- ✓ Get out the handbook and read it.

✓ Avoid drugs and alcohol.

✓ Limit your alcohol consumption at a work party, perhaps by being the designated driver.

✓ Stop other people from making a serious mistake if you're in a group.[11]

✓ Before you 'push the button' ask yourself: what will you say to your partner when you arrive home after having been unexpectedly dismissed?

✱ SUMMARY

Avoiding Technical Knock Outs is a sensible way for us to keep our jobs and it's surprising how many ways there are to fall foul of the regulations. Just because your supervisor says that it's okay, it isn't necessarily so; you could be punished for being complicit, or an accessory to malpractice. If in doubt, consult a senior manager or someone from the human resources department. Write down your concerns and keep relevant notes and signatures.

If you think you need help to avoid saying something inappropriate, or to cope with a drink problem, then do get help. We all need to take care of ourselves and to take responsibility for what we say and what we do or don't do. Losing our job through a TKO not only causes us problems when our position is stripped from us at short notice, but it could potentially harm our search for a new one.

---

[11] Not just participation in, but also *not acting* to prevent, dangerous behaviour could be a TKO. The latter leaves you open to an accusation of complicity, particularly if you're in a position of responsibility (such as a supervisor or a charge-hand).

7

Energy for Change

– Charging up our batteries –

YOU CAN FIND NEW WAYS TO INCREASE YOUR ENERGY

When working with clients I've noticed that, before we talk about some of the things they can do practically to improve their Productivity, People Skills and PR activity, we first need to consider their *energy levels*.

It's tempting to rush out and try new things, but if we're dragging our heels, the best that can happen is a short term 'bump' in our performance, before we sink back into our usual habits. We want to achieve a permanent change and to do that we need a constant source of energy to power our activities. Otherwise, our new found vigour won't be sustained beyond the first couple of weeks. A bit like a New Year diet that's easy to follow when we're at home and then gets smartly drop-kicked into touch when we return to work and find it easier to eat sandwiches and chocolate bars, than to prepare something low fat and tasty each day.

Paying close attention to our energy levels is likely to underpin our future success, so here's an example of someone who did just that and reaped the rewards.

LUKE'S STORY

I worked with Luke when he was new to a business that had just been refloated out of bankruptcy. The business needed to make changes – rationalise its products, get out into the market, find new customers and deal with existing clients more proactively. However, the owners wanted him to focus on improving the internal environment, while they developed marketing strategies and handled the financial aspects of the business. Luke was a polite and friendly person who worked hard and was keen to make a difference, but he had failed to make any so far. To set the scene: the premises were old, the staff were reluctant to change and the machinery was in need of repair. Even the foyer was drab, brown, tired and said to visitors, 'you're welcome, but you won't enjoy it here'.

Simply saying that you will 'work a bit harder' isn't good enough to drive up energy levels and during our second coaching session I was struck by how tired *I* was and although I was listening to Luke describe the problems in the business, the urge to sleep was overpowering. It felt like I was slowly relaxing into a giant feather bed and sleep was approaching me in caressing waves, which isn't great when you're supposed to be *motivating* the client. So, with a shake of my head and a sip of hot tea, I tapped on the desk, caught his attention and stopped the session.

'Luke,' I said firmly. 'There's no energy in this room. We're supposed to be talking about change and improvement, but there's as much enthusiasm here as in a dentist's waiting room, and that is going to get us nowhere. Please stop telling me about work and tell me about *you*. What's life like?'

'Dull,' replied Luke, staring vacantly into space, 'All I do is shuttle between work and home and that's about it.'

'Don't you have any fun?' I asked.

'Fun?' he replied, like he'd just learned a new word. 'No,' he continued sadly, 'not any more.'

It wasn't hard to work out what we needed to do. We agreed to push work to one side, go for a walk and talk about what he'd like to do *outside* of work. It transpired that what he really wanted to do was to find a new girlfriend, join a scuba club and go mountain biking. But he hadn't been on a date in years, didn't own a wetsuit and lived miles away from any interesting mountains.

Rather than discussing what he couldn't do (which just helps people to stay stuck) we talked about what he *could do* to achieve all three of these ambitions. He then realised that he could join a dating agency and go out for dinner sometimes; that a scuba club might lend him equipment and that he could call his friend and arrange to go away for a weekend cycling. The amazing thing was that, as he talked, his face filled with smiles *just at the prospect of having some fun back in his life*. By the time we returned to his office, he was brimming with energy.

So much energy that we walked right passed his office without stopping.

'Come on, let's have a look round the business and I can show you where I plan to make changes,' he called out over his shoulder as we headed through the heavy fire doors and into the production zone. As we walked and talked, his performance and energy levels were visibly improved – all clearly underpinned by the mere *thought* of doing something fun in his spare time.

The next time I visited him, I was met by a cheeky smile and a twinkle in his eye, which suggested that the dating was going well. The scuba and the cycling had taken off too, but the dating was the big win for him and the lady he went out for dinner with had become his girlfriend and is now his wife. Luke stayed with the company, managed it through incredibly difficult times and was eventually promoted to become an external business consultant, helping other businesses make internal changes.

He kept his job and thrived by working hard, completing his tasks and reaching his goals. However, we both knew that the energy do to this came from the wellspring of fun and happiness that he had created for himself *outside* of work.

GET SOME WORK-LIFE *IMBALANCE*

You might be reading this thinking, 'no, surely he means get some *balance*,' but I don't. The concept of balance is a misleading one. This is because – given the amount of time we tend to be at work each week – we have a built-in *imbalance* that's incredibly difficult to correct. I have noticed that when people talk about making career changes to balance their life, they often have in mind glossy brochures of the latest pyramid scene run by Dr Doug Dubious, a tanned 50-something with a Jaguar car and a 2-hour working week. In a society composed of billions of people, these quasi-celebrity-MLM-gods make up a tiny proportion of the population and they give *false hope to people*. They conveniently forget to mention that they have worked like fury to get to the top – we only get to see them at the pinnacle of their success and not during the years of hard solid graft that actually went into achieving it.

Secondly, balance is difficult to maintain, whereas keeping things *happily imbalanced* is a piece of cake. Here's a demonstration: take a piece of cake – any cake will do – and try and balance it on your finger so that it stays in mid air. Now simply put your finger on the table and lay the cake across it. Which is easier? The imbalance, obviously. Keeping things in a state of imbalance requires a lot less effort than keeping them balanced. Yet it can still provide us with enough rewards to make a difference.

Trying to keep things balanced almost always ends up taking more energy to manage the system than we get out of it, so therefore, we can aim for an *imbalance* because a small investment in energy is enough to have a huge impact on our AVE scores and drive up our Organisational Impact Score. We can get an imbalance by working hard *and* by making sure that we at least have one day away from work each week (such as Saturday). Or we can devote at least four hours a week to pursuing a hobby or activity that we look forward to and enjoy having fun.

HOW TO INCREASE YOUR ENERGY

Any kind of *change* that we have to carry out in order to keep our jobs requires *more* energy than we're currently investing in the *status quo*. This can itself be draining. Here are some ways that clients have approached this issue and changed aspects of their life to increase the amount of energy they bring to work with them each day:

1. **Embrace the idea of 'fun'.** This can mean lots of different things to lots of people. You know how you like to have fun – just do a bit *more* of it. I find listening to music on the drive to work lifts my mood more than the generally depressing news does. If you like having play time with your children then set aside one extra hour for them each week, or make sure you're home to read them a bedtime story. All that kids really want is our time and our love and in return they share their energy with us.

2. **Date!** If you're single, a night out with someone lifts your game a bit and is a fun thing to do. My client Luke was nervous at first and we talked through how he could make a start in a safe way. This included using a local agency that he had used previously and really trusted.

3. **Dine out.** I'm not suggesting restaurant food here; simply inviting a friend to go out with you once a week to a bar or a café gives you something to look forward to and will put a smile on your face. A fun breakfast can make us smile all day and knowing we have afternoon cake to look forward to can keep us motivated when we're tired.

4. **Play sport.** Physical activity is well documented for increasing our levels of serotonin, which in turn boosts our mood and lifts our confidence.

5. **Play a musical instrument.** If you're not a sporty type then bashing drums, thrashing a guitar, or scraping a violin is a great way to get yourself moving.

6. **Eat breakfast.** How many of us grab a coffee and a doughnut on the way in to the office and then snack at mid-morning? A good breakfast doesn't mean eating fried food either; slow energy-release food such as oats and bananas are more likely to help keep our energy levels up. The motto from many health experts is: 'breakfast like a king, lunch like a lord and dinner like pauper.'

7. **Book a short break.** Simply having something to look forward to – like a long weekend away – can increase our energy levels. It doesn't have to be expensive either – visiting friends and having a good meal can make a world of difference.

8. **Reduce our working hours.** By this I mean cutting back on 'presenteeism' activity – where we work late or turn up super early (or do both) just to convince the boss that we're 110% committed to the cause. We will come back to this in a minute.

9. **Join a club.** Do something that interests you, whether its photography or fishing, dancing or diving, knitting or needlework.

10. **Go to bed earlier.** While that might feel like we're six years old again, the cumulative effects of a lack of sleep can be devastating. Although opinion is divided on the exact amount of sleep we need as a minimum, a good rule of

thumb is to aim for seven to nine hours each night. Sleep restores our energy banks and increases our ability to stave off infection. It also gives the body time to repair itself and to file memorable events from the previous day. Go to bed earlier for three nights in a row and see how good you feel. If that is hard to achieve, try employing a 'sleep-Wednesday' tactic – go to bed earlier on Wednesday every week and allow yourself to catch up a bit with your sleep debt. Even if all you do is lie down quietly or read, you're still resting your body. People I've met who say that they can't sleep because they're thinking of things tend to have one thing in common: they're trying to remember too much 'stuff'. Take five minutes to make a list or jot down a few notes, and your brain will switch off much more easily.

11. **Less caffeine, more water.** Research suggests that because caffeine acts as a diuretic (removes water from our system) we need *three* cups of coffee to get the same amount of fluid intake as we would from *two* glasses of water. Add that to the fact that caffeine is a powerful stimulant and a highly addictive drug that can cause anxiety, insomnia, high blood pressure, urinary disorders and prostate trouble and it's not hard to see how *drinking tea and coffee to motivate ourselves is hugely counterproductive.* I'm sure if it had just been invented, it would have been banned on public health grounds. Green tea is better and water is best. I gave up coffee (which I loved dearly) six years ago. Withdrawal gave me headaches for several days while the shrunken capillaries in my brain were returning to normal, but eventually I felt less fatigued and I slept better. And I saved money.[12]

12. **Smarten up.** I've noticed that when people are struggling at work it shows up in their clothes and their hair. They look worn, creased, dishevelled and a bit unloved. A smart hair cut, a new suit, a smart new bag, a new notepad and a

[12] Caffeine has some benefits in terms of keeping us awake, but a more sustainable approach is to get more sleep and also to drink more water to keep ourselves hydrated.

new watch can all make us feel like we are making a fresh start. When we catch our reflection in the glass doors on the way in to work, we look sharp and we *feel* great. Other people may notice and compliment us and that feedback loop helps to increase our energy. At a deeper level, if we take care of ourselves in this way, it confirms to us that we are worth the time and expense, that we are valuable and talented and that we can look and feel confident. If you're not sure where to start, or are worried about money, start with changing your watch – it is something we look at all the time and choosing a new one can be exciting. I have a work watch and a home watch and the work watch has a bright orange strap. It always makes me smile when I wear it because it was a birthday present. Life doesn't have to be dull grey. If you like colour then add it to your working wardrobe – even if only through a pair of jazzy socks!

THE WORKING HOURS SCAM

Some organisations have a culture of attendance, where people who work longer hours generate more respect, because apparently they care more. This is annoying nonsense and can lead to increased fatigue, so it pays to think about what we're *actually doing with the time*, instead of being caught in the 'presenteeism' trap – where we fool ourselves into thinking that we are 'dependable-Bob' or 'dedicated-Denise', always on hand and shuffling paper late into the evening.

Many years ago I used to prepare a report of overtime requirements for a business. It required a computer programme to be run and numbers added up. I fell into the habit of staying behind on a Tuesday for an extra three hours to do it, convincing myself that I needed a quiet space to work in and pleased that my late nights meant people would see that I was taking my job 'seriously'. However, after two months of this, there came a Tuesday when I couldn't stay late and had to produce the report on the Wednesday morning. Remarkably, I managed to complete it within half an hour. That caught my attention and made me think about how I had been wasting my time before. Of course, my line manager didn't care either way; he just wanted the report in on time.

I realised I had fallen foul of that classic trap, known as *Parkinson's Law* – which states that work expands to fill the time allotted to it. If we set ourselves an hour to do a task, that's how long it will tend to take, but if we give ourselves 15 minutes, we will rush about and complete the same work in a fraction of the time. This is why people often say 'if you want to get something done, ask a busy person.'

The working hours scam is that if we eat into our evening, we reduce our free time *and* our fun time, which will make us more tired the next day. This means that we are less productive and will have to stay late to catch up. Also, people know we stay late so they give us more work to do, which keeps us at our desks. We smile with pride at being one of the 'good guys' that care. However, I've never met anyone who has kept their job because they worked late. Sometimes a bit of extra effort is required to cope with peaks in workload and that is fine, but the scam is to think that if we do it all the time we are getting more AVE points for it. We're not; we're just making life harder for ourselves and the law of diminishing returns kicks in – a bit of extra effort earns us a couple of points perhaps in the short term, but more and more effort doesn't *keep* earning us more and more points.

SUSAN'S STORY

Here's a true story of someone who beat the scam. A friend of mine was in trouble at work for underperforming and for having excessive sick leave and so she asked me what she could do differently. We looked at her contracted hours and the hours she actually worked and I noticed that she was regularly being asked to attend early breakfast meetings and then work a full day, which was far in excess of what her manager had agreed she could do. She was also staying late to catch up with paperwork and because people knew she would be in her office after hours they would often pop round for an 'informal meeting'.

When we looked at the whole picture, Susan realised that she was working *against* herself – that the extra hours were a major factor affecting her health and performance. To resolve the situation we role-played a conversation and then she talked it through with her manager, showing him the facts and reminding him that she needed to stick to her hours. Otherwise her health would never recover. Also her early meetings could be covered by a colleague who preferred to work an early shift. Her line manager agreed that she could go back to her set hours for a month to give her a chance to improve and that, in return, he would be grateful for some flexibility for important meetings.

She agreed to this, on the basis that a longer day would be followed by a shorter day, to keep the total number of hours within a weekly maximum and to reduce the risk of *cumulative exhaustion*. After three weeks of sticking to the agreed work pattern, her productivity had soared, her health had largely recovered and she was getting consistently good feedback about her work.

Susan was successful because she had re-contracted with her line manager to get control over her hours, had been proactive in managing them and as a result had seen her energy levels increase dramatically. Simply by noticing the patterns, giving herself more free time and by talking it through with her manager, she had taken care of herself and beaten the scam. Her line manager didn't mind either, because instead of grumbling about her, he was now praising her and pleased that he had helped her to become more successful.

PLEASE CHOOSE

My invitation to you is to choose *one* thing that you can do to increase your energy levels. When we do something to take care of ourselves in this way, we set ourselves up for success – we gain the ability to increase productivity and improve our interactions with people. It's a bit like going on a long car journey when you don't know where the next petrol station will be – would you prefer to start your journey with a full tank of fuel or a half empty tank?

✳ SUMMARY

Increasing our energy is vital and there are practical *active* steps we can take. The secret is to take positive actions that result in some kind of physical activity, or an increase in time spent with people in *fun* situations. While I'm a big fan of 'thinking', the truth is that '*thinking* fun' doesn't make much of a tangible difference; we need to be '*doing* fun' to generate enough surplus energy to make changes at work.

Two easy steps are to cut back on the unpaid overtime at work and then to invest the time into something that makes you smile. You can be just as committed to your job and taking care of yourself is a smart move. While this might seem counter-intuitive when we want to be seen to be working hard, we need to remember that there is a difference between 'being at work' and 'being *effective* at work'. A small change to reduce the former and to increase the latter can make a noticeable difference and that's worth having.

Measure It & Manage It

– If you can see it you can sort it –

YOU CAN MONITOR YOUR PERFORMANCE

People running organisations tend to talk in numbers. They like numbers because numbers are great at telling stories. How much money are we making? How much cash is in the bank? How are sales progressing? What is the trend? Are we making our customers happier? Do we have enough numbers? These are questions that people love to ask and they need numbers to answer them, often with the help of snappy graphics and 3-D charts that are pleasing to look at and which keep us awake during important, but dull, meetings.

We can borrow from this approach and simplify it for our purposes because I've learned from my Lean process improvement work that *if you can measure it you can manage it*. This is because *if you can see it you can sort it*.

If the numbers are there for us to see, they give us useful information, help to tell a story and demand our attention. That's why we need to know our AVE scores and our Organisational Impact Score; they concentrate our thinking.

THE HAPPY CHART

Using numbers to help people keep their job began with Luke, whom we met in the previous chapter. In order to keep him focused on how high his energy levels were, I sketched a crude graph and pinned it to the wall in front of his desk, so that he could keep it in sight. Each morning his task was to score himself for how he felt that day: zero for fed up and listless and 10 for happy and bouncy. At first the score line zigzagged around the 4 – 5 mark and gradually it increased to a steady 7, which in relative terms is a 40% increase; a major improvement. The idea was not to be too worried about the score, but instead to notice whether the line was generally going up or down. Having the graph in front of him ensured he couldn't ignore it and reinforced the message that he needed to have some fun outside of work, in order to come into work with a spring in his step. He ran the chart for a couple of months and we didn't add any labels to it, because having a 'Happy Chart' on the wall seemed potentially embarrassing, so we decided to keep it a secret. To his staff it was another graph and they assumed it was about productivity. However, it became the most important graph on his wall and a central part of his effort to increase his performance and keep his job.

NOTICE THE TREND

The sad thing with most numbers that are collected in an organisation is that they are dead; they relate to events that happened in the past and are simply comments about what happened yesterday – they have no interest in what might happen tomorrow. Even our AVE scores and our Organisational Impact Score fall into this category because having great scores on a Monday might imply that they will still be great on Friday, but it doesn't guarantee it. Therefore, we need to include in our portfolio of useful tools a handful of relevant graphs which show control limits, designed to prompt action if the trend goes too far in the wrong direction. This approach makes the picture a *forward looking* one and gives us the opportunity to take corrective action *before* we plough into the ground and self-destruct.

Numbers on their own are interesting, but isolated; we need to see the trend so that we can manage our situation more effectively. That's why Luke had a 'Happy Chart' – it told him when to put in more effort and when to relax a bit, because trends give us a valuable early warning system.

Pause for a moment and look at the cartoons below. Who would you rather be like?

THE DASHBOARD

A dashboard is a device that groups several performance measures in one place. You may be familiar with the idea of a dashboard from driving a car, or as a management technique to keep useful numbers together, so that you can easily see how a business, or a piece of machinery is performing. However, how many of us have ever used a *personal* dashboard? Following the success of the Happy Chart, I now encourage clients to keep regular scores for themselves. In one case, a client would email them to me once a week and I produced the graphs, which we then used to prompt a conversation about how well he was doing, or to flush out if there were issues that needed discussing.

Producing a dashboard is simple, easy and cheap. You can either set up a spreadsheet, if you like things to be neat and tidy, or you can grab a piece of plain paper and sketch them out. There are no extra marks here for making things multicoloured or complicated – we just want to have something that works for us and is simple and reliable. So if you have a habit of over-complicating things – STOP! Just keep it simple. Also, we only want to measure the things that are personal to us, which in the case of Luke was just his happiness. Trying to measure everything is generally counterproductive, because that approach gives us so much information it blinds us to the key levers we need to work on.

When using a dashboard, the key to success is to do four things:

1. *Notice* if the trend lines are going down.
2. *Take proactive steps* to move the numbers up.
3. *Seek help* if you feel that you're getting stuck.
4. *Treat yourself* for doing well.

Here is a suggested two-week dashboard which covers the key areas we need to focus on in order to keep our jobs. The scales for the Productivity, People Skills and PR reflect the AVE score table. The other items are measured on simple 0-to-10 scales.

TYPICAL DASHBOARD

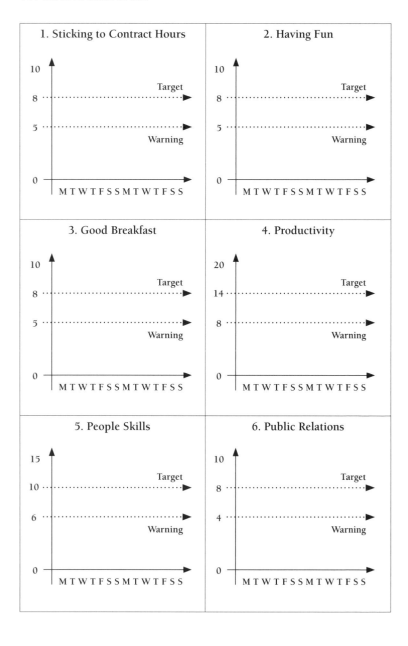

AVE Scores at the start of the first week:	Organisational Impact Score:	AVE Scores at the end of the second week:	Organisational Impact Score:
Productivity_____	P_____ x	Productivity_____	P_____ x
People Skills_____	PS_____ x	People Skills_____	PS_____ x
PR_____	PR_____ x	PR_____	PR_____ x
	Divided by 3,000 = _____		Divided by 3,000 = _____

SCORING THE DASHBOARD

The dashboard is designed to run for two weeks and then be replaced with a fresh one because having two weeks together gives us a greater sense of continuity and means that we can better include weekend working or different shift patterns. The scales have been altered to reflect the fact that Productivity, People Skills and PR have different weights, whereas the others have 0-to-10 scales to provide a general picture.

If you want to swap the title of a graph for something else, you're welcome. I've used items that are easy to score, relevant and keep cropping up more regularly. With the hours scale you score more highly for sticking to your contracted hours and lose points for slipping into unpaid overtime.

When you're scoring your own dashboard, the best thing to do is to follow your instincts, rather than spend hours consulting tables of 'what makes a 10' and so on. For example, if you've had a filling nutritious breakfast, including a drink and some time to digest it all, then that might easily rate a 10. If you ran out of the door chewing on the remains of a chocolate bar you found in your coat pocket, that probably merits a 1.

To give a greater sense of validity to your scores, please stick to the following basic guidelines:

1. Be consistent with yourself.

2. Don't award points if you haven't really earned them.

3. Score good and bad performance honestly.

4. Don't be unduly harsh on yourself for tiny mistakes.

5. Don't score yourself lower through false modesty. Good scores are good scores!

6. It is possible to score the maximum and minimum on each scale.

7. The target line is what we're aiming for. We want to be on it or above it.

8. Scores that zigzag up and down between the lines are fine because they reflect natural variations that we all experience each day.

9. The warning line means take action *now*, if we fall on it or below it.

10. If you get stuck then find a friend or get your partner to complete a sheet and compare the two. You might be surprised at how well you're doing.

ENJOY THE RIDE

The dashboard is here to bring together useful parts of our working life into a clear picture for us to see, because if we can measure it then we can manage it and if we can see it we can sort it. If you want to decorate your dashboard with comments, or change the targets, or add in an 'earn a treat' marker in week two then feel free to do so – the important thing is to make it useful and fun. It's a key tool to help us keep our job and so we *want* to use it – make it dull and, chances are, we'll never update it.

✳ SUMMARY

The dashboard is there to keep us focused on what matters and you can change the graphs around if you have your own preferences. There is a duplicate blank one in the 'Kit Box' section at the end of the book for you to use. Be honest with yourself when scoring and notice the trends and patterns: if the lines are going up then all is well and if they're going down then *action* is needed.

If you don't feel comfortable scoring yourself in isolation, then find a close friend or trusted colleague or partner and ask them also to keep scores for you. You can then compare them once a week, discuss what you're doing well and what you need to focus on next week. Remember too that health and energy are vitally important for success and that healthy food, proper relaxation time and an early night today can underpin your success at work tomorrow.

Productivity Part 1

– The art of clear contracting –

YOU CAN TAKE TIME TO CONTRACT

If there is one useful secret to great productivity that people need to know then it's this – if we take time to get a clear contract for our work, we significantly increase our chances of success. I know this to be the case because whenever a client complains that he is in trouble at work and doesn't know what to do, my first question is always: *What's your contract?* Almost every time, the client can't answer that question because they have never given the idea of *contracting* a moment's thought and do not have a contract to work towards.

If we want to become *Added Value Employees*, we need to know that the main ingredients to high-performing productivity are:

- clear *contracting*; and
- consistent on time high-quality *delivery*.

If we can master these two essential disciplines, then we're a long way ahead of our colleagues and well placed to become truly high-performing individuals. This chapter looks at clear contracting and the next one at consistent delivery.

THE NEED FOR CONTRACTING

Getting a clear contract for our work is something both fundamentally important and consistently overlooked, simply because many people are not aware of the need for it. What we mean here by 'contracting' is to discuss the work and its outputs and agree what is going to be done, by whom and for what deadline. We need to have a clear contract for each task, because if we don't, we could waste time, make mistakes, or miss unseen deadlines. Having a clear contract sets us up for success because we will deliver our work:

- to the right standard,
- in the right quantity; and
- at the right time.

Not having a contract is like setting off for a desert adventure without a map, a compass, or a wristwatch. We will certainly have an adventure of sorts, but we are likely to end up lost, or even dead. If we don't know what the contract is, how do we know if we're on track for success, or are heading towards certain failure?

ALL AGREEMENTS ARE CONTRACTS

We often think about contracts in 'big' terms, such as our contract of employment, a marriage contract, or a contract to buy a house. In work terms, every time we *agree* to go to a meeting, fix a piece of machinery, type a report, serve a customer, lead a team, or solve a problem, we are contracting. Even though most of our contracts are verbal and quick, that doesn't mean that people aren't relying on us any the less. This is easily tested – arrive home for dinner two hours later than your partner was expecting you and see what happens!

Contracts can be agreed in minutes or days. They can be written and they can be verbal. However, they *always* establish a set of expectations for our performance and we need to be mindful of that.

HOW TO CONTRACT

Knowing how to contract is a vital skill that we need to have in order to become *Added Value Employees*, yet it's likely to be a skill few people in the office possess. How often do you talk about contracting at work? Probably never. If you're lucky, you might have had a conversation about meeting *expectations*, but this is often limited to an annual appraisal and often relates only to high level objectives and outcomes. With contracting, the key is to remember that everything can be contracted for – delivering a piece of work, holding a meeting, going to see a client, 1-to-1 reviews and performance discussions, organising work teams and setting daily tasks and targets.

Contracting is a *process* and is often an *iterative process*, which means that we need to keep revisiting it until all parties have clarity. In order to make sure we have addressed all the key parts of the process here is a 7-step approach that breaks contracting into useful chunks of activity:

7-STEP CONTRACTING PROCESS
1. Check
2. 2W+WHW
3. Competency
4. Reality Check
5. Set way-points
6. Add some contingency
7. Re-contract

THE 7-STEP CONTRACTING PROCESS IN DETAIL

1. **Check.** When you have a task to do, ask yourself if you're clear what the agreement is about – or indeed if you have one that is mutually satisfying. If you have any doubts, then you don't have a clear contract and need to say to the other person (or people), 'We need to contract for this.'

2. **2W+WHW.** We need to understand the parameters that define the work. Spend as long as you need to agree the *what-1, what-2, who, how and when* of the task:

   a. *What-1* – 'What are the outcomes of the task, in measurable terms?'

   b. *What-2* – 'What is the expected quality standard?'

   c. *Who* – 'Who is responsible for doing the work?' (This may require additional people to be involved in the contracting process.)

   d. *How* – 'How is the task going to be done?' (Think about resources, room space, tools, equipment that's needed.)

   e. *When* – 'When is the drop-dead date?' (The deadline that must not be breached.)

3. **Competency.** This is a big catch for lots of people. We need to ask ourselves if we are competent to do the work in question. Do we have the skills, or the time available to do the job to the required standard? If we are working with a team, do they have the right skill level? Asking someone to 'create a spreadsheet' or 'draft a presentation' sounds like an easy task to contract for and yet I've noticed that lots of people who don't use tools like Excel or PowerPoint regularly are often not able to achieve the required standard. Once we agree to the contract, we become responsible for it and over-estimating people's skills is a sure fire way to cause problems later on.

4. **Reality Check.** Take a mental 'step back'. Review the answers to all the above questions and ask yourself if this

piece of work is actually deliverable? Plenty of people have been caught out by agreeing to a contract that in their hearts they knew to be at best tight for time, or at worst undeliverable. All too often, people have a sense that it's going to be hard to achieve at the start and yet they continue with it. If your feeling is that the contract is flawed in some way, then stop and re-negotiate where you need to. It's always better to ask the 'silly questions' now than to leave them hanging the air.[13]

5. **Set way-points.** A way-point is a milestone to be reached that helps the task to be broken down into smaller stages, with points of review at the end of each stage. Having agreed check-in times will help to keep the work on track.

6. **Add some contingency.** Often a contract is by its nature flawed, because it's trying to pin down unknowns. This is like forecasting the weather; we might know *roughly* what the weather will be like next week, but we're often wrong at *detail* level. If you accept that (1) people work at different speeds on different days, (2) you can rely on the 'unexpected' to happen and (3) the world of employment rarely follows a steady course, it makes sense to incorporate *some spare time* into our contract. For example, if we know that it will take three weeks to write a report and we contract to have it completed in three weeks, it's likely that 50% of the time we will fail because of the nature of variations in output. However, if we add two days as a contingency and contract to include that flexibility, we will dramatically increase the likelihood of delivering the report on time.

7. **Re-contract.** Seldom is a contract properly worked out in the first pass and it's only after doing a portion of the work, or reflecting on the size and scale of the task, that people are aware of the actual real-world boundaries on resources, timescales and personal performance. Good contracts are

---

[13] The only 'silly questions' are the ones we don't ask. Asking questions costs us nothing.

formed and *re-formed* as the work progresses so that all parties know clearly what is going on and what is going to happen in terms of the end-point delivery.

BEWARE OF OVER-SPECIFICATION

When we contract to do something it's tempting to agree to supply more than someone needs, or in our heads to think that we'll add extra items for extra praise, but if we want to use our time effectively it makes sense to make sure we are adding value and *not* adding padding. For example, I used to write a lengthy and detailed board report each month and thought I was working to a high standard, until my director pointed out that it was interfering with other duties and wasn't all read anyway. When the board asked for a one-page summary that's what they meant; one page. So, as a result of this chastening experience, I learned to ask these two simple questions to keep me focused on the important things:

- What do you really want?
- What's the acceptable minimum you're looking for?

Asking people what they *really* want enables them to separate the important things from the 'nice to have' items and focuses their thinking on what really adds value for them. Asking for their acceptable minimum sets the standard which we need to attain. We need to be effective at work and not waste time over-delivering if there is no added benefit, because the law of diminishing returns applies – if we keep adding more and more, we end up with less and less benefit. A bit like over-decorating a room: we go from bare, to decorated, to looking great, to looking cluttered, to a confusing mess. Work is the same, and with clear contracting we can give ourselves attainable targets to reach.

CONTRACTING QUESTIONS

Often the essence of clear contracting is to ask great questions, as they promote discussion, invite people to think and unlock potential. Here are my favourite ones and my suggestion is simply to learn them so that you can recall them when you need them:

TEN GREAT CONTRACTING QUESTIONS
1. What's your priority?
2. What is likely to cause me a problem?
3. How soon do you really need it?
4. What does success look like?
5. Who can I get to support me?
6. Who do I need to talk with to make this happen?
7. How could we get this really wrong?
8. What are your key issues?
9. What is the budget for this?
10. What have you been thinking about already for this work?

These questions are designed to reach into your line manager's mind and find out what he or she is thinking and what their concerns may be, because bringing concerns to the surface now means they can be addressed. Budgets are often overlooked and are a key constraint, so if you're embarking on a larger piece of work, it pays to find out about the money. Also, asking your manager for their thoughts is a good way to get information because they may have already solved a few of the problems, or come up with pitfalls which they can share with you.

USE YOUR INSTINCTS

Clear contracting requires us to be assertive and disciplined, which, when we're feeling vulnerable, can seem like a big thing to ask for. If that is the case for you, a safe starting point is to *recognise where you have doubts* – or lack information – and simply *trust your instincts* to ask a few questions and clarify the situation. Some projects will require a lengthy contracting process, while others will be contracted for in two or three sentences. Both approaches are okay and both are equally valid because the contracting process simply brings shape and structure to our world.

DEADLINE OR DIE

This may sound a bit dramatic, but if we don't know the timescale we're working to, then we can really cause ourselves a problem because we are likely to set our own deadlines, which are seldom going to be the ones our line manager was expecting. I learned this the hard way when, during an appraisal, I had the following conversation with the director I reported to:

'Richard, I'm scoring you two points out of five for meeting deadlines.'

'What?!' I spluttered indignantly, 'that's not fair. You never set me any deadlines!'

'Yes, I know that, but you're still late!'

It turned out that when he said 'as soon as possible' he meant 'tomorrow'. Being a busy administrator, I took him at his word and tended to deliver things *the following week*. I had done them 'as soon as possible', but had set my own deadlines and therefore worked to a flawed contract.

✴ SUMMARY

Clear contracting is at the heart of high productivity because it sets us up for success. By following a simple process and asking useful questions we can find out what people really want us to do, when they want us to do it and if there are pitfalls or issues which we need to know about.

When we are working to become *Added Value Employees*, we can value ourselves and can take the time to get our contracts straightened out. This may only take a couple of minutes, but it can shape the course of the next couple of weeks or months, so it is time well spent – *time that protects us against future uncertainties* because a good clear contract gives us safety and security by providing clear boundaries for us to work within.

Productivity Part 2

– The 3Rs of productivity –

YOU CAN CHOOSE HOW TO INCREASE YOUR PRODUCTIVITY

To be *Added Value Employees*, we need to do what we've been paid to do. No *ifs* no *buts* – if we don't earn our money, we are in danger of losing our jobs and rightly so. I know that lots of people have a friend 'who has done virtually nothing for twenty years and has never been made redundant', but within the general population these oddities are very much in the minority. These people are not to be used as roles models, because they may be sleeping with the Big Boss, be related to a share holder, or be the only person who knows the combination to the office safe. In short, their line manager knows that they're useless, but the organisation has decided to keep them on for reasons which tend to be beyond the wit of ordinary decent folk who just want to work hard and keep their job. The world of work is an odd place and sometimes it is neither fair nor understandable. However, we need to rise above this and assume that we have no special privileges. We need to know the secrets of success and here is the second slice, after clear contracting – high performing people deliver the *3Rs of Productivity:*

> **THE 3Rs OF PRODUCTIVITY:**
> 1. Right Quality
> 2. Right Quantity
> 3. Right Time

In the previous chapter, we looked at the how to contract and in this one we will focus on smart ways to deliver the goods *on time every time* by concentrating on the *essential* techniques that people have used to make a difference.

CONSISTENCY

When we deliver our work it needs to be *on time, in full and to the right standard.* The phrase 'on time in full' means exactly that and is well known to people who work in manufacturing environments, in terms of making sure the products reach the customer when they are meant to. If we want to keep our job it means that we need to build a reputation for being reliable, because having one good week, followed by one bad week, is a 'zero sum' – they cancel each other out.

When we score our dashboard for productivity we need to aim to be consistent. This can be affected by the amount of sleep we're getting and the energy we're bringing to work each day. To be consistent we need to keep the contract in sight, make sure we have enough energy to do the work and pay attention to the other tips that follow because they all work in harmony to improve our performance.

FOCUS

Following on from our awareness about the need to keep delivering on time in full, we need to pause and make sure that we are doing the right tasks. It's very tempting to do everyone else's work and be seen as being helpful, but we'll get little thanks for it if our own work is suffering. Also, we may get sidetracked by an overflowing inbox that seems to demand our constant attention, with the result that at the end of the day we have worked very hard, but have achieved very little.

> **MAINTAIN YOUR FOCUS BY:**
> 1. Remembering Pareto
> 2. Replacing 'no'
> 3. Producing a 4-hour list

1. Remembering Pareto. Vilfredo Pareto (1848–1923) was an Italian engineer who became a celebrated economist at the University of Lausanne in Switzerland. In 1906 he observed that in Italy 80% of the wealth was owned by 20% of the population and this was later generalised into the *Pareto Principle*.[14] If you produce a chart of customer complaints, for example, it's likely that 80% of complaints will come from only 20% of the categories. Or, if you analyse the cash owed to a business it's highly likely that 80% of the total will be owed by 20% of the customers. This insight

---

[14] This term was coined by Joseph Juran around 1941. Juran was an influential management consultant who wrote about quality and quantity management. He often referred to the 80/20 Principle as 'the vital few and the trivial many'. This was later adapted to the more reasonable 'the vital few and the useful many'. We need to focus on completing the vital few tasks and keeping the useful many in sight.

is useful to us because it's highly probable that 20% of our tasks contain 80% of the value, or that if we work for 100 hours there will be 20% which contribute 80% of the value-added output.

Knowing this means that we be tough with our to-do list – we must consider which are essential tasks that add the most value, and which are the 'nice to haves', which don't. The value-adding tasks are generally the ones that either earn money, save money, save processing time, or enable others to make a similarly useful impact. Tasks which are essentially maintenance, or housekeeping, tend not to add as much value and need to be pushed down our list of priorities.

2. Replacing 'no'. When someone asks you to do their work for them and you know that really you should say 'no' but can't bring yourself to do so, simply replace it with 'not yet'! This is a polite way of acknowledging their request and leaves the door open for doing it later, by which time they would have found someone else to do it for them anyway. You can say 'not yet' and save yourself a lot of time. It's assertive and it works.

3. Producing a 4-hour list. The third task is to write a very short to-do list that you think will only take about 4 hours to complete. In order to focus, we need to have clear minds. This means reducing the workload in our mind, because if we attempt to do too much, we will fail. The secret is to focus on completing an achievable set of tasks today and then to start something we had planned to do tomorrow. This creates a *pull system*, where instead of constantly being stressed by our lack of apparent productivity we feel great at reaching the end of our list and can feel that we're ahead of tomorrow.

The next day, write another small 4-hour list. Do not exceed the 4-hour limit. Studies tend suggest that we are only productive for about *five* hours in an average eight hour working day, once you factor in breaks, chatting, slow performance and random interruptions. Even five hours can be an over-estimate when we look at how much output we have actually delivered, so four hours is a sensible number to focus on. Once we're focused it's amazing how much work we can complete and once completed it's off our backlog. Completion is important because we add more value by achieving a few fully-completed tasks than we do by having many half-completed tasks.

CHOOSE TO BE ACTIVE

This is a subtle point and easily overlooked when we want to keep our jobs and are worried. Often we find ourselves wandering round in a little circle, particularly if we come up against a task that we're just not sure how to tackle. We want to be productive, but we're stuck and we know it. What happens is that we invest our energy into staying stuck, perhaps to the point of deep frustration or even anger. We blame others for letting us down and we curse the world for our lack of progress because we don't have the parts, the time, the support, the knowledge, the money… the list of excuses rattles on. Notice though, that we have the energy to complain; we're not comatose here – we are *choosing* to invest our energy in this way. This is a common trap that people can fall into.

There is an easy way out:

✓ **Invest your energy into *constructive* activity instead.**

Instead of thinking about what you can't do, think about what you *can do*, however small it seems. That is one step away from being stuck and one step towards getting back into your flow again. By way of an example, Lindsay was stuck. She knew she had to complete a detailed analysis of customer complaints for an insurance company, but the person who was supposed to be working with her had moved to another department. So Lindsay was on her own and unsure of how to complete the task. She had already gathered a few bits of data, but was now fretting that time was slipping away and that she was getting nowhere. She rang me and asked if could help her. I offered up a couple of useful questions to get her thinking again. These were:

- Who else could you go and talk to?
- How soon could you talk to them?

She thought about it and remembered that within her own office, there was a woman who was a spreadsheet expert; she would probably know what to do. Talking to this particular colleague hadn't occurred to her before because that lady was engaged on a different project in another part of the organisation, and was hardly ever at her desk. Lindsay telephoned her and she readily agreed to give her the support she needed. Lindsay also discussed her plan with their line manager, who was pleased that she was being proactive. He had been worried that she was stuck and had been wasting her time.

Being active begins by allowing yourself to wake up to the fact that you're stuck. Any piece of work which is really frustrating you and not progressing is a stuck piece of work. It means that you're investing energy in *staying* frustrated. Stop pouring your energy into going nowhere by talking to somebody, because talking helps us to unlock our thinking. We can know three things for sure:

- Asking for help is what *Added Value Employees* do.
- Being resourceful increases our productivity.
- We always have other options.

We can choose to stay stuck or we can choose to do something to move us forward. Every time we curse and feel blocked, or frustrated, we *are* making a choice. Stop making the same choice and make a *new* choice – talk to someone, find some options and get moving again. We'll often discover that even if we don't know someone who can help directly, we do know someone who knows *the* someone who *can*.

STOP TRYING AND START DOING

More often than not, the people who are not producing the required levels of productivity have fallen into bad habits and are rushing about *trying* to be everywhere at once and *trying* to please everyone at the same time. They might also be procrastinating and are confident that tomorrow they will *try* to make a new start. Notice the use of the words *trying* and *try*, which have a deep significance that is often not picked up by people.

If we *try* and do something we give ourselves a little 'wriggle room' to ensure that if we don't complete it we can say that at least we had a go. We have made an effort. We started the work, even if it was a tiny and largely ineffectual start. Our assumption is that this raises us above criticism, because we can show that we did put *some* energy into the task. In reality, it simply increases the expectation that we will finish it tomorrow and magnifies the disappointment when we *try* to finish it and fail because 'something cropped up'.

Promising to *try* and do a piece of work is a con because it sets us up for not finishing the task and yet we think that we've protected ourselves with our little linguistic insurance policy. After all, we never said that we would definitely finish the report by five o'clock, we only committed to *try* and finish it by then –

often knowing full well that this was a contract we were unlikely to be able to fulfil.

Listen to your own speech and notice when the word *try* is slipped into a sentence. It means that you're not fully committed and are likely to fail to deliver on time, in full, or to the right standard. When you hear yourself say 'try', you need to stop the sentence and restate it without that word; it makes a considerable difference to our productivity because it commits us to achieving the outcome, which is what we need to do if we want to keep our job. To make the point about how much the word 'try' can sabotage good performance, consider these two alternative statements from the pilots of two different aeroplanes that you could be flying in:

- 'This is Captain Smith speaking. We're arriving at the airport now and beginning our final approach onto the centre runway. I'm going to try and land the plane safely.'
- 'This is Captain Jones speaking. We're arriving at the airport now and beginning our final approach onto the centre runway. I'm going to land the plane safely.'

Which pilot would you rather be flying with?

THINKING IS ESSENTIAL

Thinking is work. Anyone who says otherwise is either teasing, or is a blunt-minded dinosaur headed for extinction. People who have a high output don't simply turn the handle and produce a mass of unthinking, shapeless bits of information. They think about what they are doing and take time to sift and sort, draft and review, sketch and collate. Blind productivity is no productivity. However, the important skill is to recognise that 80% of the value is contained within 20% of the thinking time, so if we were to think for an hour, our most creative and incisive thoughts will tend to happen in the first ten minutes; the rest of the time is taken up with the development of these initial ideas. This means the way to be successful is to have lots of '10-minute bursts' and give our brain something to do afterwards. We will still continue to process off-line and out of awareness, which means that we can get on with another task and then review our thinking a bit later.

High performing people know that using a do-and-review process is what drives really high value output. Taking ten minutes to check our work, to stand back and survey the scene, or to talk through progress with a colleague is the move of champions. Top sportsmen and women will spend time watching videotapes of their performance to see where they need to hone a muscle, or adjust their footing – they review their progress and use that information to guide their ongoing improvement.

THINKING TIP #1
We need to think widely and consider assumptions, alternatives and options. We need to think deeply about the consequences of action and inaction. We need to ask ourselves if we are meeting the contract, or if we have drifted off course, or whether the contract has shifted in some way.

- **The Silent Brainstorm:** If we work with a team then we can invite people to think by holding a silent brainstorm – this is where you pose a question and give your colleagues two minutes in silence to note down their responses. Silence means silence – which some people may be uncomfortable with – but with this method you will get thoughts from the whole group and not just those who shout first, or loudest.

After two minutes, ask people to read out what they have written or to pin-up their piece of paper, so that everyone can read it for themselves. Then repeat the process if you need to accumulate more ideas, as people will now have their brain 'warmed up' and will be starting to develop their thinking and their responses to other people's thoughts.

If we fall into the trap of assuming work always means *doing*, then we will notice an initial increase in our productivity, followed by a long slow decline, as we make mistakes and waste time by heading off in the wrong direction. Instead we need to recognise that work is a balanced mixture of doing *and thinking*. When we are planning our day, we need to allow time to review and think, so here is my second top tip on this subject:

THINKING TIP #2
At the end of your 4-hour list have a break and then take 15 to 30 minutes reviewing your work so far and giving yourself some thinking space. Quality thinking time adds value and creates high-performing people.

ORGANISE YOUR ENVIRONMENT

If we want to increase our productivity scores, then we need to be organised. Because if we try to cram too much into our brain we're likely to fail and will forget details, dates and deadlines. I worked with a team leader who spent much of his day rushing between meetings, whilst clutching a fistful of papers. When I asked him what his team was doing, he didn't know. Pretty poor for a team leader, who needed to be in control of his own productivity and that of eight expensive change agents.

The kit list that follows is glaringly obvious to some and yet people who are struggling to be productive often lack simple tools. They inhabit an unstructured and cluttered environment. For example, a friend of mine saved an entire hospital department from closure because she tidied it up. This may sound ridiculous, but they were swamped with packaging and old bits of equipment and even had an office that was so full of 'important documents' it had become an unofficial storeroom. One of these 'important documents' turned out to be a box of chocolates that was four years past its use-by date. The tidy-up created space and clear work-flows and, as a result, productivity soared.

Despite the rise of the i-Everything there is still a place for paper because it's cheap, simple to use and doesn't require a stack of batteries. When you're looking to improve your environment, remember to go for quick and simple solutions because 80% of the value will be in 20% of the changes you make. You can improve your productivity by having:

- **A day book.** Any kind of bound notepad will do. These are great for making notes and because they have proper binding you won't lose bits of paper as you rush about.
- **A diary.** I've never worked with a struggling manager who owned a diary and used it. I've worked with a few who sometimes looked at their intranet diary on their laptop, but they tended to consider it a nuisance rather than a tool. Whatever sort of diary you prefer to use, make sure that it's up-to-date. Schedule blocks of work for your 4-hour list and give yourself spare time to cope with those interruptions which are always guaranteed to happen.
- **A ring binder.** If you are managing a team, then carrying

individual action lists for people means that you don't have to remember them when asked. It also means that if you're in a meeting and need to find out where one of your team is with a project, you can refer to your notes. This approach increases your assertiveness because it sends a message to the team that you're not going to forget what they've agreed to do and it shows your line manager that you are in control and have a clear system for keeping important notes up to date. The manager who rushed about with loose documents decided to transfer them to a file and then added a section for each member of his team. A week later, he was praised for being in control and knowing what his department was up to.

- **A pad of sticky notes.** These are the busy worker's best friend. Use them to scribble quick notes, plan processes and keep to-do lists visible at the side of your workstation.

- **A tidy workstation.** A colleague of mine lost a customer cheque down the back of his desk and was nearly fired for it. It was only worth about £10,000 and accounts needed the cash urgently. If we have a messy desk, or cluttered work bench, we will spend half our day wading through the rubbish to find what we need. Our time is better used adding value and not wasted on searching. The same applies if you have to walk half a mile to the nearest printer or fax machine. This is also a waste of your time and if you can get one put right next to you, you can be more productive.

- **A shadow board approach.** Lots of people who use tools have a shadow board which has distinct outlines of the tools drawn on it, so that when a hammer is removed the outline remains, prompting people to return the tool to the right place. This is a great way to save time and effort because if everything has a known home, it is going to be there when we need it, instead of scattered around our workshop. If your equipment is in a mess, then take some time to sort it out: find a home for everything and label it, so that you can maintain a tidy time-saving standard.

PRODUCTIVITY PERMISSIONS

A 'permission' is a phrase that enables us to make a change in our thinking.[15] Our productivity is often constrained by what we are repeating to ourselves in our head, just on the edge of our awareness. We think that if we follow certain patterns we will be well thought of and will be safe from getting rebuked from senior managers. However, although well intentioned, some of the mechanisms we have evolved to cope with an uncertain work environment are counterproductive. An example is the person who prints the same letter five times and repeatedly checks it for spelling mistakes. Printing it once, checking and correcting it once then sending it out is quite enough. Constant fiddling and polishing wastes time and can produce a worse result, like an antique plate that has been over-cleaned, causing all the gold leaf to be rubbed off.

The following permissions have been used by people to increase their performance and they're offered here for you to read and soak up. They're all true. You can tweak the words to make

---

[15] This concept is taken from Transactional Analysis (TA), which I frequently use in organisational settings. TA is the study of communication skills and looks at how we communicate with the world around us and what we say to ourselves. You can find out more about TA from, amongst others, the European Association of Transactional Analysis (EATA) and the International Transactional Analysis Association (ITAA).

them sit more comfortably in your head if you wish to and my tip is to read them and notice which one(s) resonate the most with you. (This means that one or two will get your attention and really make sense to you – they're the ones you needed to hear. If you want to physically hear them, then ask a trusted friend to read them out to you.)

Once you have identified your helpful permissions write them on a sticky note and keep them in sight on your desk or workstation bench. They're all true, remember, and they reflect what we've already talked about in this chapter:

PRODUCTIVITY PERMISSIONS:
1. Good enough is good enough (beware of diminishing returns).
2. You can work first and then have some fun.
3. You can say 'not now' or 'not yet'.
4. You can put *your* priorities and needs first.
5. You can ask for help.
6. You can revisit the contract.
7. You don't have to know everything to be great.
8. You can take time to plan your work.
9. You can focus on the key tasks and improve your situation.
10. You can work diligently and become even more of an *Added Value Employee.*
11. You can pace yourself (instead of leaving it all to the last minute).
12. You can work at a comfortable pace.
13. You can take a break.
14. You can delegate tasks to colleagues and juniors.
15. You can listen to music and be productive at the same time.
16. You can talk to someone if you get stuck.
17. You can put your health first (because that underpins success).
18. You can get a good night's sleep.
19. You can think widely and deeply.
20. You can choose what you're going to do differently to be successful.

21. You can re-contract with your line manager.
22. You can do what you need to do today and leave the rest until tomorrow.
23. You can review your progress.
24. You can be creative.
25. You can enjoy your success.
26. You can reward yourself for being productive.
27. You can be resourceful and find new options.
28. You can be proactive and find ways to solve problems.
29. You can have gaps in your knowledge or skills and still be really successful.
30. You can be nervous and still make a start.
31. You can take time to think things through.
32. You can know when to stop thinking and start doing.
33. You can choose to meet deadlines.
34. You can set way-points and review progress.
35. You can stop being stuck and make a new choice to be active.

THE IMPORTANCE OF STAMINA

Elsewhere in this book we have talked about the need to be healthy and rested in order to turn up to work with enough energy each day to be productive. It's worth restating this. If we are worried about losing our job then we are likely to fret, allow ourselves to be distracted and may suffer from broken sleep and a poor diet. All of these are natural stress responses and we convince ourselves that another slice of comforting pizza is what we need. It isn't. If you were a footballer and worried about being dropped from the team for lacklustre performance, what would you do about it? In many ways, we're all footballers and we need to:

- Drink less caffeine and more water.
- Eat less processed food and more of a healthy balanced diet.
- Spend less time in the pub, wine bar or social club and more time sleeping in bed.

- Spend less time slumped in front of the television and more time exercising. (A brisk 15-minute walk once a day means you'll walk an extra 350 miles or so each year. Swimming is good too if you have a pool near you.)

✱ SUMMARY

If we want to increase our productivity, we can. Often our success depends on being healthy and organised, and focusing on *completing* key tasks. We can use simple and effective techniques to achieve this and we can choose what to concentrate our efforts on.

We can give ourselves permission to be more productive and can jettison unhelpful behaviour and old ways of thinking in favour of new choices. It's up to us to be responsible for our own actions, be powerful and dramatically increase our productivity.

We can decide which items in this chapter will make the most difference to us and we can put them into practice right away, because we know the difference between trying to do something and *actually doing it*.

So, here's a good question to leave you mulling over: when you reflect on this chapter, *what's the biggest change that you can make today that will make the biggest difference to you?*

People Skills

– How to communicate effectively –

YOU CAN BE A SKILLFUL COMMUNICATOR

In my experience, many people lose their jobs simply because they don't communicate effectively with their line manager and their colleagues, and become branded as 'difficult to deal with'. These poor souls might be technically excellent, but they lack the confidence to communicate in assertive and meaningful ways, so when the time comes to get rid of people they are in the firing line. Although managers may choose to keep someone who is a nuisance if they have a high work-rate, these leaders tend to be in a minority and most people are quick to seize an opportunity to redeploy people who are part of the 'awkward squad'.

Although the world of people skills is broad and deep, interestingly there are often just one or two key changes that we need to make in order to be thought of as a skilful communicator. This chapter contains the most frequently used tips and things to change and as you read through them, choose one or two that would be most useful to you. Focus on getting them embedded into your everyday positive work habits. Once this has been achieved, the others will tend to flow in around them, so our task here is to focus on the 'vital few.'

VALUE YOURSELF

Many people give themselves a negative self-talk when they are under stress, such as:

- 'It's ok for her; she has more qualifications than me.'
- 'I'm no good; any moment now I'm going to be found out as a fraud.'
- 'He hates me.'
- 'I'm stupid really.'
- 'I shouldn't be here.'
- 'I'm not good enough.'

And so on… as if we can read people's minds and know exactly what they're thinking about us. Can you really read minds? Really? We say these things to avoid disappointment when we do get 'found out' because secretly we knew all along that we didn't deserve to be there and can understand our employer making us redundant. Wrong. Wrong, wrong, *wrong!* If we think like this then we are going to become a *Self-Fulfilling Prophecy* (an SFP), which means that we *think* ourselves down, so we *talk* ourselves down, then we *act* down and eventually *fall* down. This is surprisingly, and sadly, fairly common and it shows up when we interact with other people. Our chin goes down, we don't make eye contact, our tone of voice is fairly quiet and we let our shoulders sag under the load they carry.

I have some news for you.

You are great. You have skill and talent and, in your life, will have achieved things that other people are envious about. They may not seem much to you – because society often encourages us to be modest and therefore we're not used to singing our own praises – but that doesn't mean you're not a valuable worthwhile person. Also, if you've worked hard to achieve something it will feel normal to you and so is easy to overlook. To an outsider though, what is normal to you is special to them. Instead of giving ourselves a negative talk, we need to build up our self-esteem, and that will help us excel in people skills.

> **PEOPLE SKILLS TIP**
> This is what we need to say when we're feeling stressed:
> - 'I have a right to be here.'
> - 'I can choose to think.'
> - 'I am a valuable person.'
> - 'I can make changes.'
> - 'I can find my voice.'
> - 'I can find a good way to make myself heard.'
> - 'I have talent, both when I'm talking and when I'm quiet.'
> - 'I can take a deep breath and then make a start.'

If we 'talk ourselves up', we are likely to feel more pride in our hearts. Don't forget that, at the end of the day, in any organisation, we are *all* good people. Therefore, we must always remind ourselves that we have value, are great and can communicate effectively.

KEY COMMUNICATION SKILLS

What follows is a list of simple and effective ways for us to assert ourselves in a confident, friendly and non-threatening manner. Effective communication stems from getting the small things right, because we are very good at noticing tiny clues in our peripheral vision which convince us either that the other person is worth listening to, or is wasting our time. Once we have our positive self-talk in place, the next step is to decide which skills we need to practice. For each of the skills below, score yourself out of 10 and notice which you do well and which you need to work on.

1) Smile with your eyes
Low 1 – 2 – 3 – 4 – 5 – 6 – 7 – 8 – 9 – 10 High

Stretching your mouth into a curve is not a smile; we need our eyes to crinkle a bit in order to tell the other person we really mean it. If you're struggling to mean it then a good tip is to remind yourself how the other person could be of help to you, or to remember a time when you liked him or her (even it was only at your recruitment interview). Triggering a happy memory will trigger a genuine smile.

2) Keep your head up
Low 1 – 2 – 3 – 4 – 5 – 6 – 7 – 8 – 9 – 10 High

If you wear glasses and have a habit of looking at people over the top of them, or you address people with your chin tucked into your neck, it mimics a parent bending down to a small child. This tends to convey 'I'm better than you', or 'I'm in charge here.' This is often learned behaviour that we carry with us without realising. If this concerns you, get your glasses adjusted so they sit firmly on your face, or keep your chin up and make eye contact!

3) Keep your head straight
Low 1 – 2 – 3 – 4 – 5 – 6 – 7 – 8 – 9 – 10 High

If you've ever been accused of being patronising, it's a fair bet that when you're talking you let your head tilt to one side. This behaviour is copied from a time when we were little – when someone took care of us and would tilt their head whilst soothing us with: 'Ah, there there, mummy will take care of it.' As grown-ups we may be *trying* to be helpful, but because our body language looks a bit like a mother, the other person may feel overwhelmed and resent the intrusion. In the same way we used to when we asked mum to help us with our homework and her form of helping was doing it *all for us*, instead of simply answering the technical question we had. If we keep our head straight and give the other person the help they *ask* for, people won't feel like they are being smothered in cotton wool, or talked down to.

4) Use the 'snow plough'

Low 1 – 2 – 3 – 4 – 5 – 6 – 7 – 8 – 9 – 10 High

When we want to move people around, perhaps to get them to sit down or to leave a meeting room, instead of pointing at the door, or waving our hand at them dismissively, we can *use our palms*. Stand up with your arms hanging down by your side with your palms facing forwards. Then when you want to move people, push gently with your hands as if you're moving the air between you and them, which is a cue for them to move. This action looks a bit like you're moving a wall of snow and it works because people detect the gesture in their peripheral vision and it reinforces your spoken command, such as 'Shall we please move back to our desks now?' Practice this as it's an assertive way to move people without pointing.

5) Put the gun away

Low 1 – 2 – 3 – 4 – 5 – 6 – 7 – 8 – 9 – 10 High

People point as if they're waving a six-shooter about, like a cowboy in a Western. Fingers are for holding pens, pushing buttons, or for keeping in pockets. Pointing with a pen is just as bad – people don't like being poked across the desk either.

6) Hold eye contact

Low 1 – 2 – 3 – 4 – 5 – 6 – 7 – 8 – 9 – 10 High

Looking at someone is a really great way to make your presence felt and let them know you're listening to them. When it's your turn to speak and you want them to really hear your message, hold their eye contact for a count of three… such as *one-two-three*… then *look away*. Most people find a count of two is enough for general conversation, so the third 'beat' underscores your message. If you smile whilst you're talking, then they will feel you are assertive and friendly.

7) Listen with your face

Low 1 – 2 – 3 – 4 – 5 – 6 – 7 – 8 – 9 – 10 High

Active listening is much talked about and seldom practiced and you cannot really pay attention while you're tapping on your smartphone, or gazing at the ceiling, or running an internal dialogue about what you're going to have for supper. To be effective we need to focus on the other person. However, because we can't twist our ears about to show that we are listening, we have to use our faces. We can arch an eyebrow, make eye contact, wrinkle our forehead, nod gently, smile broadly and say 'uh-huh' and 'okay' and 'I heard that'. Looking down and making copious notes is not a good way to listen, as we miss every second word. If we pay attention and only write down the occasional key word, people will feel valued and they will like us for that.

8) Make small talk

Low 1 – 2 – 3 – 4 – 5 – 6 – 7 – 8 – 9 – 10 High

Good people skills means being good at the work bits *and* the social bits, so if you have a habit of walking into an office and just sitting down and getting on with things, people may think you're being rude. This happened to me once when I was deep in thought and my colleague scowled and said, 'What's up with you, grumpy?' 'Nothing,' I replied, 'I was just thinking.' Instead, I should have said, 'Hello,' and asked how his weekend had been. Noticing people in this way is a friendly and constructive thing to do because we all have a need for recognition, and this needs to be constantly topped up. Small talk might be frustrating sometimes, but people need it, in the way they need little snacks to keep them going throughout the day.

9) Use their name

Low 1 – 2 – 3 – 4 – 5 – 6 – 7 – 8 – 9 – 10 High

Many years ago a friend of mine wasn't getting on with a colleague and so talked it through with a close friend. The close friend noticed that, during his conversation, this friend of mine had a habit of referring to the colleague as 'him in finance'. Not using a name and instead greeting someone with a blank 'hi' cuts away at a person's self-esteem. It can even hook feelings of anger and resentment. (Calling people *mate* can be just as bad.) The solution was to suggest that the next time they met, he started the meeting by shaking hands, saying, 'Hello Ed,' and asking him about how his working day was going. He did this and was surprised that, instead of the usual sour greeting and abrupt discussion, his change paid off. Ed was polite in return and they fell into a fun conversation.

10) Apologise if you mess up

Low 1 – 2 – 3 – 4 – 5 – 6 – 7 – 8 – 9 – 10 High

When was the last time you apologised for your behaviour at work? If you get cross or interrupt someone, or glare at your colleague before sweeping off in a huff, then you have *bruised* them. It's the behavioural equivalent of thumping them on the arm, because they have to absorb your emotion and they can't do anything about it. You may have good reason for feeling aggrieved and that is fine. However, most people leave the wound unhealed, saying that it was 'just a one-off'. The truth, however, is likely to be that you have overlooked many other little 'one offs' you have had last month. If you apologise for your behaviour and are sincere, it tells the other person you are taking responsibility for your actions and gives you a chance to have a restorative conversation that enables you both to park it. Otherwise, you will risk being labelled as a 'difficult person to work with' and difficult people are often shown the door. Apologising is assertive and if you talk through your frustrations, the conversation will be productive rather than blameful.

11) Wonder aloud

Low 1 – 2 – 3 – 4 – 5 – 6 – 7 – 8 – 9 – 10 High

If you want to make a point, sell an idea, or find out what's behind someone's comment, don't begin by apologising for your 'silly' idea. Don't mumble your thoughts, or stay silent either. Instead, try prefacing your comment with 'I wonder…'. This is an assertive way to make an enquiry because it's non-judgmental and invites other people to think. For example, contrast these pairs of statements:

- 'Why did you suggest that idea?' and
  'I wonder if you'd tell me what's behind your thinking?'

- 'My turn to make a suggestion here. We should build it *this* way,' and
  'I wonder how it would be if we built it *this* way?'
- 'Look, this meeting is getting nowhere and you're all wasting my time,' and
  'I wonder what the real issue is here as we seem to be a bit stuck?'

If we were having a conversation, which would you prefer to hear? Notice how, although each statement in the pair is making the same point, the ones beginning with 'I wonder...' have a different emotional content and are framed as reasonable questions, to encourage the disclosure of useful information.

12) Ask short questions

Low 1 – 2 – 3 – 4 – 5 – 6 – 7 – 8 – 9 – 10 High

Lots of people spend time telling others what to do, instead of asking questions to get them to think more for themselves. Although a 'telling' style can be useful, if overused people get fed up with being dictated to. Executive coaching experience suggests that the best results come from short, purposeful questions. Also, if we insert the word *really*, it invites us to think at a deeper level. Closed questions have a defined answer and are good for reaching a decision. Open questions, on the other hand, invite a more general response and are good for fact finding and revealing information. We can use them both to good effect.

CLOSED QUESTION EXAMPLES:
- Shall we complete the task now or later?
- Do you have five minutes to spare today or tomorrow?
- Which machine would you like me to fix first? A, B or C?

OPEN QUESTION EXAMPLES:
- What are the facts?
- What do we need to have achieved by the end of the meeting?
- What options do we have?
- Who do we need to talk to?
- Where do we want to begin?
- How shall we do this?
- When do we need to review the progress?
- What options do we have?
- What *other* options could we experiment with?

POWERFUL QUESTION EXAMPLES:
- When are you really going to make a start?
- Are you really going to finish that today?
- What's really frustrating you?
- What do we need to do to really get them to buy into this?
- What do you really want for your birthday?[16]

13) Ask what, not why

Low 1 – 2 – 3 – 4 – 5 – 6 – 7 – 8 – 9 – 10 High

The word 'why' is asked of parents to children and children to parents with such monotonous regularity that we become conditioned to it being a nuisance. When we use it as a grown up, it can often catapult us back to a time where an annoying parent used to ask us why we hadn't tidied our room (as if we really cared about having a tidy room!). Or it might invoke memories of your child asking: 'why is the sky blue? Why are the clouds white? Why do cows go moo? Why... why... why...?' Until we lose it and snap back: 'Because I say so!' Instead of using why, use *what* instead and notice how much more friendly the other person is

[16] I include this question as a friendly reminder that all of these techniques and skills can be easily practiced at home and are not only for use at work.

towards you and how much more useful information you get out of them.

14) Choose relationship over task

Low 1 − 2 − 3 − 4 − 5 − 6 − 7 − 8 − 9 − 10 High

What this means is that sometimes we might crush someone with our forceful drive or our intellect, in order to get the job done. While this is great for today, it leaves people feeling bruised and battered and they may label us as 'uncaring' or 'aggressive' for our tough attitude. Sometimes it pays to put the relationship first, because there will always be another task, but you may not get a chance to work on it if you're let go of before then. Practical ways to put the relationship first include asking other people for their opinions, listening to their genuine concerns, finding out what they're worried about, taking a time-out to cool down, backing down so you lose the fight and win the war, pausing the conversation to review the facts and working on something else for a while.

15) Be nice to people

Low 1 − 2 − 3 − 4 − 5 − 6 − 7 − 8 − 9 − 10 High

Nice is a word that gets a bad press, because it seems so vague and nondescript, which is a pity because it's a perfectly agreeable term. Being 'nice' to people means noticing when they are looking smart, making them a cup of coffee, offering help if they're struggling, asking them about their health or holiday, including them in conversations, turning the music down if it irritates them, offering to do the washing up, being approachable and sociable and remembering that you are part of an organisation and not a little island which can repel all tourists and interlopers. Being 'nice' isn't about being 'fake' or assuming that one bag of doughnuts makes up for six months of moodiness. It's about consistent, even-handed friendliness which brings a warm feeling to people that you're a *nice* person to have around. People buy people and they buy the people they like.

16) Use a 'pause' button
Low 1 – 2 – 3 – 4 – 5 – 6 – 7 – 8 – 9 – 10 High
Sometimes we have something to say and need to assert our presence in order to take control of the conversation and create space for us to speak. This can cause difficulty for people who struggle to balance speaking up with being 'polite'. The way to overcome this is to use the pause button technique, which is simple to learn and highly effective. When you want to speak, put your hand out flat, palm down as if you are resting it on a large soft button and as you do so, say 'Can I just pause you for a moment, please.' You're now in control. You haven't asked the other person to 'shut up', you've simply put them on hold for a moment and can now say what was on your mind. Once you've finished, smile and say 'thank you for listening, please continue.' You can then push the button again to click it *off* pause. This is a great technique to use and if you don't have a table near you, you can hold your hand out, palm down, in mid-air and keep it still.

17) Notice fatigue
Low 1 – 2 – 3 – 4 – 5 – 6 – 7 – 8 – 9 – 10 High
Using effective communication skills requires energy and alertness. Often we have the most arguments with our partner in the evening, when we're tired after a long day, or at the weekend when we're recovering after a long week. This is because we forget

our helpful techniques and let our fed-up side peek out and poke people. This is often okay when we're with partners, because they love us and tolerate us. At work though, we can lose points for poor performance and may even get disciplined for a severe out-burst. Think about when you tend to flag during the day and then take steps to take care of yourself. For example, don't schedule meetings that will run into these 'tired zones' because you're increasing your chances of getting grumpy. Make sure you eat something at lunch time, and be aware of the post-lunch dip when we feel tired as our body burns energy to digest the food. If we start to feel tired we can stop and get a glass of water, open a window, go to the bathroom (even if it's just a socially acceptable way to give yourself breathing space for five minutes), or pause the conversation and ask for a break.

18) Notice irritation

Low 1 – 2 – 3 – 4 – 5 – 6 – 7 – 8 – 9 – 10 High

Often when we get tired, we get irritated. Also, when the conversation heads off in a different direction and we feel snubbed, we get irritated. When we feel that we're right and they're wrong, we get irritated. At these times it's highly likely that we will display some kind of agitated behaviour, such as drumming our fingers, tapping a foot, clicking a pen, grinding our teeth, or attempting to speak without actually speaking. Skillful people notice these clues and do something to take care of themselves, because if we leave them to fester, we risk an angry outburst that will be unproductive. The first thing is to notice what we do when we're irritated. And then recall that we always have options we can exercise to avoid speaking in haste, which include:

- Counting to ten.

- Taking three deep breaths, exhaling slowly to calm ourselves down.
- Shifting our position in our chair and giving our shoulders a little shake as we do.
- Taking a deep breath and using a 'pause button' to make ourselves heard.
- Asking to be excused for a moment and then going to for a short walk.
- Playing with a piece of sticky-tack or folding up a piece of paper.

We need to do something physical to release the pent-up energy that is driving our irritation forwards and finding something to play with is more constructive than drumming our fingers in a repetitive fashion. Good communication skills need to include ways of coping with the stress of being irritated, because we don't want to undo any of our good work from implementing the other tips and skills.

19) Let it go

Low 1 – 2 – 3 – 4 – 5 – 6 – 7 – 8 – 9 – 10 High

Sometimes, we spoil relationships by picking at something that didn't go the way we wanted. We revisit it and pore over the fine details, often to make sure we pin the blame on the right person. This creates an atmosphere where people are frightened of making mistakes and so either produce less work, or work at much slower rates as they invest time checking and proof reading. Given that most mistakes and errors are small in nature and easily solved, we need to learn to 'let it go'. We can puff out an imaginary bubble full of our angst and can let it float away, or we can scribble our annoyance on a piece of paper and then promptly shred it. We don't have to burden ourselves with this load. Let it go, because tomorrow is a whole new day and we need all of our energy for it.

20) Celebrate success

Low 1 – 2 – 3 – 4 – 5 – 6 – 7 – 8 – 9 – 10 High

This is a good way to develop great rapport with people because by celebrating success with them, we're putting credit in the bank – credit we may need to withdraw at a later date when we need them to help us out. Simply saying 'well done' or 'thank you for your hard work' can have an enormous impact if it is delivered in a sincere and genuine manner. People need feedback all the time and even the word *feed*back makes it clear that nourishment is needed. Often people remember lots of small celebrations in a better light than one big party that makes up for the whole of the last year. A working month is a long time to go without any kind of positive comments and often the leaders who provide lots of compliments, say thank you, and notice good performance, become well-respected team leaders. They get promoted. People like working for them and they work harder because they feel valued, not resented. Find ways to say well done to your colleagues, including a handshake, or some lunch, or a meal out. Thank them in front of the team, or send them a private and thoughtfully worded email. Doing these things earns points, whereas *not* doing them leaves a vacuum and breeds resentment. People can't see into our minds and they really don't know what we're thinking: we have to tell them or show them in some way.

CHOOSE YOUR AREAS FOR DEVELOPMENT

Spend a moment looking back through this chapter and identify the one or two things that you need to concentrate on most in order to have the greatest effect on your People Skills score. Then make a note of them here before you move on:

I will invest 70% of my people skills development time into doing a really great job of this:	

I will invest 30% of my people skills development time into doing a better job of this:	

✱ SUMMARY

Don't treat people as you'd like to be treated yourself, because your standards may be lower than theirs. Instead assume that everyone has value and deserves to be treated in a polite, thoughtful and respectful manner: we can notice them, look at them, say thank you and apologise to them if we make a mistake. We can be good at all the things in this chapter and we can begin by selecting the areas we most need to work on *today*.

The world is surprisingly small and well connected and with the rise of social media, the ability for people to express opinions and influence others has never been greater. Because we intend to keep our jobs by becoming *Added Value Employees*, we will practice simple techniques to use language skilfully and to increase our assertiveness. This will make us more effective communicators and we will gather praise for our people skills.

We need to keep our two chosen development areas in sight at all times and remember that every time we do well, our *Organisational Impact Score* increases.

Public Relations

– Getting your message out –

YOU CAN BE WELL KNOWN AND WELL THOUGHT OF

The third key element of our *Organisational Impact Score* – which we need to become *Added Value Employees* and keep our jobs – is Public Relations (PR). Given our rampant celebrity-obsessed culture, where everyone seems to be hiring PR professionals to squeeze their way onto the cover of a tacky tea-break magazine, you could be forgiven for thinking that PR is the preserve of the talentless and insincere. However, this is to mistake the nature of celebrity PR with that of *business* PR, which is all about people:

✓ knowing we exist,

✓ perceiving that we are talented and skillful; and

✓ perceiving that we are an asset and that we add value.

When the top managers make decisions about who to promote and who to get rid of, their decision-making will be partly based on objective assessments – such as psychometric profiles – and partly on subjective assessments, such as annual appraisals and 'gut instinct'. The world works by playing its 'hunches' and it is okay to account for emotions when making decisions if our feelings are based on *factual* episodes. For example, we may not remember all the loving things our partner may have said to us over the years, but the fact that they have said them leaves us with an emotional residue that informs our opinion of them. Business PR is the same because if we keep people informed of good news and positive contributions, they will remember a 'sense' of our contribution, even though they may struggle to articulate specific details. This 'feeling' can be a very powerful force for good and it's up to us to make sure we embed it in as many decision-makers as possible.

PUBLIC RELATION MYTHS

Whenever I raise the issue of PR, people tend to respond with either 'Ugh, that's what the greasy people do', or 'I could never do that, as I don't have the confidence'. While both of these make sense to people, they are both myths because PR is a professional, learned skill, which can be practiced and refined. One of the things that makes knowing it so powerful is that many people will tend to overlook doing it as a bit beneath them, or say 'there's no need to worry, I'll be fine'. This is usually shorthand for 'I'm scared to do anything' and we need to know that being nervous *and* being productive can both exist at the same time for us. Myths exist because of ignorance and fear and the message here is that working proactively to create positive PR for ourselves is a *necessary* part of learning how to keep our job. It's a perfectly honourable activity and, if we're sincere and friendly, there is nothing to worry about.

You can develop great PR skills that help to showcase you in a positive light. You can know too that organisations are often crying out for talented, assertive people and that sharing good news is welcomed by everyone. All you're doing is allowing the organisation to know that you're an asset. That's allowed and it's not tacky; it's a key part of giving yourself a chance to succeed. So, ignore the myth makers and make a decision to become effective at organisational PR.

WHAT'S YOUR MESSAGE?

We need to understand that creating positive PR isn't about simply shaking hands and smiling at people. We need to have a sense of what our goal is, in terms of getting our message across to people. A great way to do that is to create a *3-Word Strap Line*. Lots of businesses have a little strap line that sits under their corporate logo that aims to say something positive about them. Although many of these can often be derided as vague, clichéd, or generally meaningless, they *do* have a positive drip-drip-drip effect that sneaks past our gaze via our peripheral vision and lodges in our subconscious.

It may take a bit of time to get our three words sorted out, but once we have them, they will help to focus our PR mission, because if we aim to be 'everything to everybody' we will end up being 'nothing to nobody'. Focusing makes our message more succinct, easier to remember and more believable than a long list of adjectives that simply raise the question – surely no one can be *that* good? Here's how you create your 3-Word Strap Line:

HOW TO CREATE YOUR 3-WORD STRAP LINE

Re-read your CV, check your last appraisal and chat with your most trusted work colleague. Review your highlights, the achievements you're proudest of and the days when you excelled. Then think about what you know you tend to do really well most of the time. What do you consider some of your key skills? What have you often been praised for? What makes you feel different, or talented? Remember that 3 words sound believable, whereas 10 don't! Make a list of 15 words that you like and then ruthlessly cut them down until you have 3 which fit you the most comfortably. Examples include:

- Detailed – diligent – determined
- Friendly – thoughtful – polite
- Reliable – hard-working – creative
- Proactive – loyal – supportive
- Confident – outgoing – engaging

Notice that if you had said all of these words in one sound bite it would sound fake, but that three words together sound more focused and believable.

Once you have your three words, make sure they appear in the profile section of your CV. You could even add them to your calling card! (If you don't have a formal business card, it doesn't mean you can't carry a calling card with you – there are lots of great templates available on the internet. Carrying a card means you can give it to a new contact and they will keep your details. Cards also save scribbling your email address on a scrap of paper and they certainly look more professional.)[17]

The advantage of having a 3-Word Strap Line is that often, when people are networking and chatting to new people, they get asked, 'Tell me about yourself.' This is a question that can stump the unprepared. A simple way to answer that question in a work environment is to say:

[17] For more information on CVs and networking skills please refer to the book, *Job Hunting 3.0.*

'Well, I'm a *creative* person who likes *detail* and enjoys *supporting* my colleagues.'

Or:

'I'm an *outgoing* person who likes *listening* to customers and delivering *engaging* presentations.'

Your three words can be embedded into your answer and they will increase your confidence and assertiveness because, instead of fumbling to think of something in the moment, you will have words in your head. In addition, as the conversation develops, because they are genuine strengths, you'll have stories and anecdotes to back them up.

THE METROPOLITAN MODEL

A useful way to get a sense of progress in our PR activities is to reflect on the 'geographical area' we are covering. We can conceptualise this by moving from a small and local environment to a large and complex one, where we may be less well known, but which contains lots of new opportunities to meet people. As we want to keep our job, our target is to aim for the biggest reach within our host organisation, in order that we have the most number of decision makers in our team of supporters.

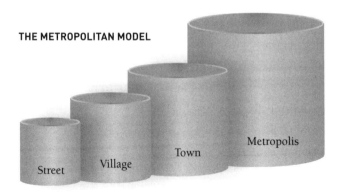

THE METROPOLITAN MODEL

Street   Village   Town   Metropolis

Street. This is where you 'live' – your immediate environment and the people you work next to every day, including your immediate supervisor, or line manager. Who do you talk to? Who notices when you're on holiday?

Village. This is the floor you're on, which may be divided into offices or an open plan office with partitions, or a shop floor full of machinery. Some of your line manager's colleagues may be here, with teams from different departments. Do you ever walk a different route to your workstation and say hello to someone new? How many people are there on this floor? How many people do you speak to every week?

Town. This is the building you work in and it may contain several managers and one or more senior managers, such as a general manager, or a director (or vice president). There may be several floors and many offices. How many have you visited? Who is the most senior person that you know? How many friends do you have in other departments?

Metropolis. This is the whole organisation, which may include the head office and other sites, which we can think of as a network of sprawling suburbs that all link up to make one large entity. At the *metropolitan* level, there is a board of directors and a managing director (or a chief executive officer, if you like your metropolis to have an American flavoured leader). How many director level people are you on friendly terms with? How many other sites have you visited? How many people in the whole organisation know you exist?

The model is there to allow us to get a sense of how far our PR has taken us into the organisation and at first sight it might seem ridiculous to think of knowing people in other locations and at a very senior level. However, the reality is that, because organisations are little networks of people, it's possible to become well known quite quickly. In my early career I was chosen to deliver company presentations to visiting customers, because I was the best at it from my team. This meant I would spend a couple of hours each month with the board, impressing our customers with technical improvement details and, because I did a good job I was asked to do more by the managing director, which was great PR for me. In another organisation, a colleague of mine was invited to support his operations director in presenting to their senior vice president from America, because not only was his work to a high standard, he was an enthusiastic and friendly person. His presentation was a great success and he made his boss (and himself) look good. Within a year he was promoted.

Many people stick at street level and never raise their gaze, or feel too timid to venture out of their comfort zone and we need to recognise that the world is there to be introduced to us. We need to explore our environment, or we could be embarrassed by our ignorance. For example, when working at a university one day, I was asked by a client if we had a department of nanotechnology. Not knowing if we did, I asked my director about it:

'Ahhhh yes Richard,' he said with a small smile, 'we do have one.'

'Where is it then?' I replied, surprised that we had such a thing.

'At the end of the corridor, Richard,' he drawled casually, 'Just through the doors.'

Whilst I was tempted to joke that a department of nanotechnology was bound to be small, and therefore easy to overlook, I was surprised to know that *anything* was beyond the doors, which we traditionally never went through. Presumably in case there were dragons and monsters with fangs on the other side. How foolish was I! Please open doors and explore your organisation, as much as you can.[18]

MOVING FROM STREET TO METROPOLIS

In order to increase our PR score, we need to follow a process of activity that gradually allows us to expand our reach by gently stretching what we do, so that each step is a small and easy one to take. PR is about creating opportunities and responding to opportunities when they arise. We can be nervous and we can get help, if we need it. The key is to *do* things, rather than just *think* about doing things, because PR is a 'doing sport'.

In order to increase our AVE score, we can work through the following activities, with the aim of taking at least one new step each week, so that we follow a manageable organisational PR process:

Getting Started

- **Write down your 3-Word Strap Line.**
- **Make a Contact Map.** Use a blank sheet of paper and write your name in the middle. Then add spokes around it labelled: friends, managers, directors, clubs, training, work-groups, volunteers and supporters (e.g. mentors or coaches). Finally, against each spoke, write the names of all the people you are connected to and those you already know well. Once you have completed it you will have a picture of how well known you already are and where some of your gaps are.
- **Read through the following options listed below.** Tick the ones that you already do to a high standard and circle the ones you need to begin doing.

---

[18] Nanotechnology is the science of building machines and formulating new materials at an atomic or molecular level. One nanometre (nm) is one billionth of a metre.

- **Plan your PR campaign.** In your diary, choose one *new* option for each week and write it in the margin. When you reach that week, you will then see what you need to be doing.

Section 1 – Street Level PR

- **List everyone whom you work in close proximity with.** Whose birthday do you know? When did you last get them a cup of coffee? Who do you never speak to? If you don't like someone, do you need to make more of an effort and find out a bit about them? Often we make our enemies first and our friends second and just because you don't get on with someone today, it doesn't mean that a possible friendship isn't waiting to spark into life.
- **Generate a chain of good news.** When you have achieved something that you're pleased with, be sure to tell your line manager. A two-line email is all you need. They will smile when they read it and will probably mention it to *their* line manager, because it shows what an effective leader they are. If it's a significant success, the good news can travel up the organisation and you start being seen as someone who creates a positive contribution. We need to realise that being *seen* is essential. Aim to create at least one good news email every week. Most people never mention good news, so you will stand out.
- **Be nice to your line manager.** Managers are people too and thanking them for their support, or for their clarity in setting objectives, is a pleasant and engaging way to work with people. Plus, it creates a good feeling about you.
- **Be known for being reliable.** Nothing sabotages good PR

quicker than a person who turns up late, is suspiciously sick after every Bank Holiday and who offers to make the tea and yet never quite gets round to it. Consistency counts as it sets up a sense of reliability at a deep level and we are trusted by others. Honour your promises and keep to the rules.[19]

- **Invite your manager on a progress tour.** Many managers overlook what is happening in their own department because they have so many things going on for them, so they become blind to improvements and changes. At the end of every month, invite your manager to spend ten minutes with you and show him what has changed and what you have improved. This is a friendly way to share your progress. Managers who *see* your successes are more likely to remember the details because people remember experiences more clearly than if they're just told something.

- **Support changes and new initiatives.** All organisations need to keep improving or they will be overtaken by competitors. When change happens it's tempting to grumble and be obstructive, often without good reason. If you have issues, then find out the facts that support them and discuss them with your manager in a friendly way. You can be seen to be supportive and have questions at the same time. Simply being cross and making a fuss is a great way to ruin your

---

[19] People do notice when a colleague repeatedly takes single days off sick, because the chances of having influenza on Monday and being miraculously cured by Tuesday are slim. The chance that you then get a 24-hour stomach bug six weeks later and then have a one-day toothache the month after that is just too much to believe. If you're sick, you're sick, but be wary of single-day sickness as many organisations know that there is a high chance you're really skipping work. People look for patterns and notice how some staff use single-day sickness as a kind of holiday-top-up. Don't do it; it undermines your personal PR and could get you sacked.

personal PR and just because your best friend hates change, you don't have to follow him. Be seen to embrace the need for change to generate positive PR for yourself.

Section 2 – Village Level PR

- **Be interested in other people.** Vary your route back to your desk and, when an opportunity presents itself, smile to people as you pass by. When they smile back, stop and introduce yourself and ask them a prepared question, such as:
  - *Are you having a busy day?*
  - *How long have you worked here?*

  A two-minute conversation is enough time to build rapport and then you can invite them back to visit your department, as people are often interested and yet don't feel that they can simply intrude. Having an invitation from you is friendly and breaks that barrier.
- **Ask questions at meetings.** If you go to a meeting, make a point of chatting with other managers and share good news with them. Be interested in their departments and ask if you can visit to find out more. People feel good when they're explaining about their projects and technical skills and as a result they will feel good about you asking them. Being interested doesn't mean being insincere; it's about wanting to learn more as the more we know about how the organisation works, the better we are able to do our job. During the meeting, you can ask questions to help clarify facts and can suggest alternative options, as this is assertive and adds value to the decision-making process. If you're not feeling confident, remember to start your thoughts with 'I wonder if…'

- **Offer help to people.** Even if they don't accept it, you still create a good feeling in people because you've established the expectation that if they should need support you're a good person to ask.
- **Let's do lunch.** Invite people to meet up for a snack and offer to treat them, as a friendly way to spend time together. I've noticed that inviting people to meet up to talk business feels dull, but inviting them 'to do cake' is more engaging and has a higher success rate, because it sounds fun and relaxed, even though business often forms part of the conversation.
- **Carry your diary.** When you're talking to people and arranging meetings, always carry your diary and snap it open so that you can capture a time and date there and then. This is a good test of their commitment and once things are written down, they're more likely to happen than if you leave the arrangements to be sorted out at another time.
- **Be proactive when on sick leave.** I've noticed that senior managers don't mind if people go sick – what they mind about is a lack of performance, given that their focus is on the delivery of objectives. When people are sick, they're rarely asleep for 24 hours a day. So, if you're off sick, make sure you take at least one hour per day to email your team, ask about their progress, delegate tasks and remain in the discussion loop. Keep your line manager informed of work-related progress, so that they know you are still providing leadership and are in control, even though you may be physically absent. When a senior manager used this approach, his new line manager was delighted that he was able to take time off to get better *and* was able to keep his team organised and delivering outputs at the same time. On

the day he came back to work, she met him and was full of praise for his proactive attitude.

Section 3 – Town Level PR

- **Ask for a mentor.** Having a senior level mentor is a great way to get to know a director, because it's a legitimate thing to ask for and it gives you time each month with them on a formal basis. A mentor is there to help provide support in terms of understanding the organisation, checking out your thinking, developing leadership or technical skills and making sense of the corporate strategy. Always aim to get the most senior person you can, in order to have the biggest reach into the senior echelons of the management hierarchy. Your mentor is there to help you develop, so it doesn't matter if you have skill gaps, or make the odd mistake. What counts is what you do about it. I often say to people that having a mentor is like having a corporate insurance policy; when things get difficult you can talk to your mentor, who will want to help you if you have a good working relationship with them. They can also bypass some of the management *malaise* if you need a lift, because they have influence and can open doors for you. A good way to get started with a mentor is to schedule meetings for your lunch hour and to buy them some food in return for their time. Make it easy for them to say 'yes' to your invitation to be your mentor and to do the work at a sensible time, so that it doesn't intrude on their busy day.
- **Apply for internal jobs.** Even if you have some doubts about the job, by applying for it you become *visible* and you get talked about. You look committed to the organisation,

keen to make progress with your career and ready for a new challenge. The process of sorting out your CV and going for an interview builds confidence and then, when a job is advertised that you really want, you're much better prepared for it. Also, you never know what other roles are being discussed and once you're seen as someone who wants to get on, an organisation may find a new role for you. This happened to a client of mine who wanted to move departments at a large service business. She applied for several roles and discussed her ambitions with a senior manager, who was happy to support her development. Although she didn't get the first couple of jobs that she applied for, her senior supporter encouraged her to continue applying and steered her towards a previously unknown opportunity. She secured the role, moved to a new department and was soon promoted.

- **Explore the building.** Call people and ask to visit their department. Be interested in their work and use it as opportunity to make new friends.
- **Attend training courses.** If there are internal courses then go on them and increase your reputation as someone who likes to learn new skills and polish existing ones. Keep a note of people's email addresses and contact them afterwards to stay in touch and invite them for lunch. Becoming known as someone who likes to learn increases our PR score and our credibility, particularly if we wish to be promoted.

Section 4 – Metropolitan PR

- **Volunteer for groups.** If your organisation has Quality Circles, or a Health & Safety Committee, or a Christmas Party Organising Committee then volunteer to become a member. Many of these groups are cross-functional and will be led by a senior manager, so taking part does two things: it puts you in front of senior people and you become seen as someone who adds value. Often these groups struggle to find new members, so volunteering helps people out and you become the kind of person that the organisation likes to have around.

- **Identify key stakeholders.** Review the organisational chart and identify the managers and directors who may have an influence on your department. If they're internal customers, treat them as customers – hold regular performance reviews and respond proactively to their issues and frustrations. If they act as suppliers, find out how you can make their life easier for them.

- **Take part in charity events.** Lots of organisations sponsor charity events or organise fun runs and the like. Taking part brings you into contact with new people and gives you the chance to make new friends.

- **Join social clubs.** If your organisation runs a club that you're interested in, then join it and have fun.

- **Attend events.** Going to summer barbeques and Christmas parties can sometimes feel like a day wasted, but they're an opportunity to be seen and to chat with colleagues in a social environment that's relaxed and friendly.

- **Visit other sites.** If you have colleagues in similar departments in other locations then go and see them and learn about what they do well and where you can make improvements in your own department. Inter-departmental bench-marking is a great way to get out and about and it helps you to be seen as someone who wants to keep improving the business.

- **Be opportunistic.** Switch on your 'PR radar' and notice opportunities to meet people, be part of groups, spread good news and get your message out. You can contribute to the works magazine, read notice boards to see what is going on, attend conferences and then present back to your colleagues afterwards, or simply share useful information. Do take part in the life of your organisation with a smile and a friendly face!

A GOOD PROCESS BRINGS GOOD OUTCOMES

The list of PR options above is comprehensive and is designed to enable people to build a solid base of goodwill at a local level and then to find ways of spreading their reach and influence throughout their organisation. By choosing to do just one new thing each week, you will be surprised at how much you will achieve within a couple of months and taking small steps makes the process of building good PR more manageable. The outcomes are that we get to know people and they get to know us *and* like us. This is an important part of becoming an *Added Value Employee*, because, as my PR colleagues often say, 'success is all about who you know.'

✳ SUMMARY

We can all be good at organisational PR and it's a worthwhile and useful skill to develop. If we want to keep our jobs, then we need to establish our presence within the organisation and become known to the decision makers. We also need to be recognised as people who like to learn, are in favour of change, have value adding skills and attributes and who deliver their work on time and to the right standard.

Being known as reliable and consistent means that we can build up our PR score from a solid foundation of excellence. Given that an annual appraisal can be a long time in coming and quick to be forgotten, we can't wait for set piece activities to create good ripples of positive PR. Instead, we need to be proactive and share good news, contribute to the general life of the organisation and *make it easy for people* to like working with us and want to have us as part of the team.

We don't have to become super-employees who always smile and are stereotypical images of perfection. We can be a normal person going about our work. The key tasks we have to complete are to accentuate the positive and share good news and successes, so that senior executives know we exist and know that we add value.

And if the thought of dealing with senior managers and directors fills you with a sense of dread, then the next chapter is there to help you and to put the record straight.

Dealing with the 'Big People'

– They're just people –

YOU ARE IMPORTANT TOO

Julie was having trouble with her work, at a hospital, because she had become trapped in a little whirlpool of only talking to people at a similar level and avoided the senior managers and medical consultants. Faced with the prospect of having to engage with the consultants, she had decided that it was safer to sit in a quiet back room and run more reports, to make doubly and trebly sure that she had all the right information before going to see them. Terrified of dealing with senior people because they had skills and qualifications that she did not possess, she wound herself up by telling herself that they were the *big* people and surely they would find out that she was 'just a *little* office worker'.

Being scared of the 'big people' is quite common because we can invest them with magical powers, x-ray vision and the ability to destroy us if we make a mistake. Of course, I know this may sound fanciful to some of us, but who hasn't sat up straight when the managing director walks into our office unannounced? Or blanched when the telephone rings and it's the group vice president on the line, asking us to come and talk to the board next week and explain the progress we've made with our mega-project?

It's normal to feel a bit apprehensive, but if it gets in the way of our progress, we need to deal with it, or we're going to be stuck in the back office like Julie.

TAKE BACK YOUR POWER

The first thing to do in order to overcome any fears about interacting with senior management is to stop investing them with super-powers and to take hold of your own power instead. Senior managers may be bright, they may have a degree, an MBA and/or significant technical qualifications. Or they may not. Many senior people I've worked with are there because they are good at what they do and not because they have a wall full of certificates.

You are bright too and not having the same qualifications doesn't make you stupid. It just means you have different interests and have chosen to spend your time differently. Indeed, many top entrepreneurs have fewer qualifications than you might expect, because often they began their businesses at an early age and focused on developing them, in preference to continuing their formal education. If you have a great point to make – or a super product to sell – people will listen to you because of the quality of what you're saying, and not because you can wave a bit of paper at them. Take back your power by pausing for a minute and reflecting on these comments:

TAKE BACK YOUR POWER BY KNOWING THAT:
Senior managers…
- Do not have x-ray vision
- Do not have magical powers
- Will not destroy us if we make one mistake

Senior managers…
- Have worries like we do
- Want the organisation to improve
- Need to identify and work with talented people

Because…
- Senior managers are under pressure to perform
- Senior managers report to someone too
- Senior managers also get fired if they're no good

Taking back our power means recognising that we are just as good as the senior people in our organisation because, without us, there is no organisation. We are all worthwhile people and we have skill and talent too.

DIFFERENTIATE YOURSELF

I talked with Julie and we listed all the things that made her a talented person in her own right, the reasons she was hired in the first place and, crucially, what she had that the consultants did not. Spotting the differences between people is a great way to boost our confidence because it is okay for us all to have unique combinations of skill, talent and positive behaviours. In Julie's case, she realised that without her help in analysing the numbers and suggesting practical ways to improve their patient flows, they were probably not going to meet their performance targets for that financial year. Realising that they *needed* her was a breakthrough moment because it enabled her to properly realise that she *was* important.

She had different skills and her contribution was needed to improve the organisation. Without her, the 'big people' were in danger of themselves getting criticised by the 'even bigger' people!

BIG PEOPLE SLEEP TOO

A payroll officer I worked with used to say this whenever the phone rang and I was summoned to a meeting with one of the engineering directors who ran the company. Being a junior, I used to feel very nervous and worried that they would consider me a 'fraud' – that they would realise I only had limited knowledge of the subject. She would remind me that we all slept and that, outside of work, we're just people who are no better or worse than anyone else.

Of course I wasn't a fraud; I was good at my job and my worry was based on false assumptions. It was a relief to find out during a meeting that one of the engineers didn't have a clue about how we ran the payroll and I realised that seniority does not necessarily imply expertise or breadth of knowledge. We can also appreciate that often we do all lead very similar lives, eating the same food and watching the same television programmes. Most cars are the same too at a functional level and when you're stuck in a traffic jam everyone is late, regardless of who made their car.

JULIE'S HAPPY ENDING

After talking with Julie, she made some changes. She decided to let herself know that she was important and that importance had no grounding in salary, or qualifications, or job title. It's about a mindset where we see the world as it really is and not in a fairytale or fantasy way.

Feeling more confident, Julie set up a meeting with the

consultants and took her reports with her. During the meeting the consultants were themselves cautious at first (who's important now?) and as they read and digested the information, clearly worried about having to make changes, there was much muttering and stroking of chins. After a long pause the senior consultant looked at Julie and broke the silence.

'This is great stuff,' he said smiling, 'we didn't know any of this before and will need your expertise to implement the changes.'

'Oh, thank you,' Julie replied, blushing, 'of course I will help you.'

✳ SUMMARY

Knowing that the big people are just people and that we all have an equally valuable contribution to make in the organisation is an essential part of underpinning our productive PR activity. It also means that we are less likely to become tongue-tied when faced with a potentially intimidating situation and are more likely to operate effectively when dealing with all levels of management. There is nothing to fear from senior managers. Often they are under enormous stress to maintain profits and meet budgets, so they welcome the chance to work with helpful, thoughtful and reliable staff.

The same people whom we might be nervous about in our organisation will lead surprisingly similar lives to us and will also worry about their mortgage, their health, or their children's performance at school. They are talented and hardworking in the same way we are and, most importantly, they do *not* have magical powers.

We can take our power and instead of using our energy to stay stuck, we can acknowledge our nervousness, see the world as it is and go and engage with them. We now know that, whatever job we are doing at whatever level in our organisation, *we are important too.*

Anchor New Behaviours

– Make structural changes –

YOU CAN GROUND YOURSELF

Reading this book and making changes today, or tomorrow, is one thing, but to maintain those improvements and build on them requires diligence and awareness. We can use the score sheets and the graphs to give us a good sense of our progress and the contribution we are making to the organisation. We can re-read bits of the book to help us to stay focused on becoming *Added Value Employees*. We can do these things and we can also make bigger structural changes to our behaviour and our environment in order to keep our new ways of thinking and behaving in view.

As we've already encountered earlier in this book, if we *try* to do things we often fail, because the word 'try' automatically gives us a little opt-out clause in our commitments. So if we finish this book and decide that we're going to *try* to remember all the good things we've promised ourselves that we will do, it's a fair bet that within two weeks, we won't remember any of them. Keeping graphs of our scores is a superb method of keeping our performance in sight and we need to be careful that, once the novelty has worn off, we do not find our daily score-keeping slipping and then having to play catch-up every Friday, trying to remember what we did during the working week that is now firmly behind us.

SHIPS AND PEOPLE NEED ANCHORS

In nautical terms, a ship needs an anchor to prevent it from dragging its mooring and drifting off into the night. In people terms, we need anchors to help us stay focused and grounded. An anchor is a physical thing for a ship. For us, too, it can be a physical thing. We can also use key phrases and words to trigger happy thoughts and restore our sense of confidence, because they enable us to pause, see the world as it is and regain control over our fears and our surging adrenaline.

CALLUM'S STORY

A very senior manager, called Callum, had to make big changes to the way he worked in order to keep his job. The new operations director he reported to had left him in no doubt that although he was a talented person, his actual performance was too inconsistent for him to be kept on in that role in the organisation. Having 'flashes of brilliance', as his director described it, was a sign that Callum had the potential to really excel, but his consistency of performance was such that if he didn't improve and maintain such improvement, he would be leaving the organisation and his ten-year stay there would be over.

Callum heard the message and was determined to do what was right in order to keep his job, because his director had made it clear that if he *could* stabilise his performance, he would become a highly valued member of the senior management team. In order to make the leap in performance that was required, Callum re-contracted with his director, kept daily score sheets for his hours worked and for his performance and telephoned me once a week for a coaching session in order to share his progress and keep things in awareness.

However, on realising that our coaching contract would end and that Callum needed to perform on his own, we discussed various options for making physical changes to his working day, in order to firmly anchor the new behaviours, and to make sure he did not regress back to his more haphazard levels of prior performance. After giving the issue thoughtful consideration, this is what he did:

CALLUM'S OPTIONS FOR ANCHORING IMPROVED PERFORMANCE

1. Change your desk. Either move things around, buy new equipment, or relocate. Callum realised that his desk was away from the central team hub in a different building and, therefore, he missed key conversations and wasted time walking to and fro. Co-locating with key colleagues meant he had new and different conversations and was firmly placed at the centre of the action.

2. Change your route to work. If we walk the same path we always get to the same place and if we've become a bit stuck in our ways then it helps to approach the organisation from a different direction. Callum chose a new route to work that took him past a new coffee shop, so he treated himself to a coffee on the way in each day.

3. Change your clothes. Wearing the same old clothes in the same way sets up an expectation that today will be the same as yesterday and we don't want that to be the case. Callum even changed the way he wore his clothes – he stopped wearing ties and began undoing his top two shirt buttons. A small change, but he now felt more relaxed and less constrained. The physical change then percolated through to his thinking.

4. Change your self-talk. We've noticed how what we say changes our thinking, such as knowing 'I have a right to be here' and 'I can take care of myself'. Callum chose to write these words on the inside cover of his diary, and his first task each day was to repeat them to himself three times. Repetition tends to cut a new groove in our conscious mind so that the words become firmly embedded.

5. Change your grip. Instead of gripping a pen with frustration and drawing small circles on a pad of paper, we can anchor ourselves by gripping our wrist with one hand and noticing the sensation of our fingers on our skin. Callum chose to do this whenever he was feeling under pressure in a meeting and instead of shouting at people (through frustration) it gave him time to break the cycle of frustration-anger-inactivity-shouting. He would listen to the chatter, whilst he discretely held his wrist under the table. Then he would ask a question to get some words out in a calmer way.

6. Change something for yourself. You can also find a way of making the change personal by ignoring all the options given above and by deciding to do one thing that is just for you. Callum's favourite anchor was a new silver rope-style neck-chain which he bought after two weeks of maintaining his contracted hours and watching his performance scores increase and stabilise. The chain was a reward to himself for two weeks of great performance and he wore it to signal that the change was permanent. He had, quite literally, invested in himself and invested in his own future.

What would you really like to do for yourself?

ANCHORS REALLY WORK

In Callum's case, the anchors made a clear difference to him because the nature of an anchor is that they don't require any special effort to maintain. They reinforced his commitment to a new way of working, made it very difficult to slip back into bad habits and seeped into his subconscious. Six months after he had started to use them, he told me a story about how he was sitting in a meeting and feeling exhausted after a long day of back-to-back meetings.

Where previously he would have become agitated and would have snapped at people, on this occasion he sat back and held his wrist until the need to snarl had subsided. He then used the pause button technique (as described in the *People Skills* chapter) to take the lead in the meeting, which allowed him to share how tired he was (noting lots of nods of agreement) and bring the meeting to an amicable close.

✳ SUMMARY

Long term success can be built on the simplest of things – knowing we are valuable, asking questions, writing 4-hour to-do lists and sharing good news with our line manager, for example. The net effect of making small changes can be dramatic because they work on the same principle as industrial hydraulics – a small movement in one area translates into much larger movement elsewhere, which has the power to move objects and lift heavy weights. In our case, the outcome is a shift in perception by our line manager, colleagues and directors.

Anchors are physical and psychological points of stability that allow us to stay centred and grounded. Instead of engaging our 'feeling brain' and blurting out nonsense, we can engage our 'thinking brain' and buy ourselves enough time to remember where we are and what we need to do next. They can be the glue that brings our behavioural changes together into one cohesive mass and they can help us to be effective long after we've forgotten what started us on our journey in the first place. Ships have changed from wood to steel to space-age high-performance metals. They have moved from wind power to steam power to nuclear power and are now sharp-edged radar deflecting stealth boats. However, they all have anchors and that has never changed – so we need to find an anchor that really works for us and make it part of our daily working life.

Time for More Action

– You've already started the journey –

YOU CAN CHOOSE HOW TO CONTINUE

This book is full of brilliant ways to improve your performance, keep your job and keep the money rolling in. You may feel a bit overwhelmed if you think that you have to do everything at once because time is against you, or because you're starting from a low base point. Fortunately, people notice small changes and, if we remember Pareto, then about 80% of our success is probably going to be contained within the first 20% of our activities. So we can relax and can concentrate on making the small changes which will bring the big rewards.

We can focus on one key area of Productivity, one key area of People Skills and a simple PR process that builds up as each week passes. We can keep our dashboard relevant to us (and up-to-date) and we can notice how our Organisational Impact Score improves over time. All of this is achievable. None of it requires a huge investment in time or resources.

We can be resourceful and use the tools that work for us. We can seek help when we need it with no loss to our personal credibility, so we can increase our confidence in manageable steps. We can make a change and review it and decide if we want to keep it, tweak it, or do something else. We can also twist the models about to suit ourselves and our particular organisation, so that they inform our thinking and allow us to personalise our journey.

AFFIRMATIONS FOR ACTION

Each chapter in this book has an affirmation at the start of it and the concept of affirmations comes from Transactional Analysis. Affirmations are similar to permissions, except that permissions tend to promote new actions and thoughts, whereas affirmations tend to promote growth and development at a deeper level and shape our sense of identity. A bit like an operator in a large signal box by the side of a railway track, who pulls the levers to change the direction of the next train, we have 'levers' in our heads and affirmations are a great way to move them from 'off' to 'on'. Here they all are again, one from each chapter. They're all true and you can know them:

CHAPTER	AFFIRMATION
Powerful You	You have more power than you realise
AVE Concept	You can be great at all three disciplines
The Value Question	You can be a valuable asset to your organisation
Practical Options	You can make changes
TKO Time	You can be smart

Energy for Change	You can find new ways to increase your energy
Measure It & Manage It	You can monitor your performance
Productivity Part 1	You can take time to contract
Productivity Part 2	You can choose how to increase your productivity
People Skills	You can be a skillful communicator
Public Relations	You can be well known and well thought of
Dealing with the 'Big People'	You are important too
Anchor New Behaviours	You can ground yourself
Time for More Action	You can choose how to continue
Kit Box	You can be resourceful

FINALLY

Here's an interesting thing – you've read the book and so have *already started* your journey towards becoming a high performing *Added Value Employee*. The next steps you take are not about starting, that bit you've already completed by arriving at this point. The next steps are simply about *continuing* the work in a direction and pace that feels comfortable to you. Everything you do that is positive is a step away from being stuck, or fed up, or worried. It is a step towards a brighter and more secure future. You can be brilliant and you can work hard to keep your job, because whatever happens in an uncertain world, you will be better placed to take advantage of opportunities and changes of direction. You're great and you can think for yourself and you can choose to make changes.

Having read the book and been encouraged along the way to choose the bits that will make the biggest difference to you, take a moment to write down your top seven choices. Writing things down increase the chances that they will become a reality, so don't be tempted to skip this bit. Think for a minute and then complete the following table:

MY KEY LEARNING POINTS FROM *HOW TO KEEP YOUR JOB* ARE:
1)
2)
3)
4)
5)
6)
7)

Then, as a final commitment to your own future, write down your next step here so that after you put the book down you know what you will be doing. Choose something simple and something that really appeals to you.

MY NEXT STEP IS GOING TO BE:

Remember Peter from the start of the book? He was stuck in a difficult situation and he made changes and turned things round and in doing so found a new level of success that seemed out of reach when he began his journey. You have the power to discover new levels of success for yourself, so enjoy the rest of your journey, enjoy being you and enjoy being a high-performing *Added Value Employee.*

Kit Box

– Models, skills, tools and secrets –

YOU CAN BE RESOURCEFUL

To become *Added Value Employees* and keep our jobs, we can decide on our own priorities and we can carry with us the kit that we know will make the most difference. We can choose the models and tools that best fit us in our situation and can tailor them so they feel comfortable to use.

This chapter is a digest of all the other chapters and gives a flavour of the brilliant tips and tools that have featured throughout this book. Think about them, use them and enjoy becoming more successful.

CHAPTER 1 – HOW IT ALL STARTED

Peter is a real person and the story actually happened. He moved from being unproductive to being an *Added Value Employee* and in doing so kept his job.

CHAPTER 2 – POWERFUL YOU

You are powerful and you can remember that:

- They chose you.
- There is always hope.
- Decisions include emotions.

We can write a list of positives and we can take responsibility for our actions. Think about key attributes and successes and fill in the table below, in any order:

Strengths I have and achievements I have made include:	Technical skills and qualifications that I have include:
1)	1)
2)	2)
3)	3)
4)	4)
5)	5)

CHAPTER 3 – THE AVE CONCEPT

Building on the criteria of Productivity, People Skills and PR, we arrive at the AVE concept because it underpins what becoming an *Added Value Employee* is all about. The concept comes in two parts: the first is to score ourselves for each of the three key areas and

the second is to combine these raw scores into our Organisational
Impact Score.

AVE SCORE TABLE	Do you do this rarely and/or badly? LOW AVE Score	Do you have good days and bad days? MEDIUM AVE Score	Do you work to a consistently high standard? HIGH AVE Score
PRODUCTIVITY	1 - 2 - 3 - 4	6 - 8 - 10 - 12	14 - 16 - 18 - 20
PEOPLE SKILLS	1 - 2 - 3 - 4	5 - 6 - 8 - 9	10 - 12 - 13 - 15
PUBLIC RELATIONS	1 - 2 - 3	4 - 5 - 7 - 8	9 - 10

NATURAL VARIATION

Choosing a precise number can feel a bit self-limiting and if this
applies to you, then recognise that although a best guess is still
valid, we can think of a range of +/− 1 place on the scales for 80%
of the time to get an idea of where our true score is likely to be
contained on most days. We can also think of a range of +/− 2
places for 20% of the time when we're either really flagging, or
over-performing.

ORGANISATIONAL IMPACT SCORE

We can work out our Organisational Impact Score by following
the simple sum below:

> **MY ORGANISATIONAL IMPACT SCORE IS:**
> Productivity score of _____ x People Skills score of _____ x
> PR score of _____ = _____
> All divided by 3,000 = _____

The number 3,000 is a constant and never varies and it reflects the maximum scores available for each category. If we multiply 20 x 15 x 10 we get to 3,000.

AVE CLASSIFICATION AND THE ORGANISATIONAL IMPACT SCORE ZONE

As an Organisational Impact Score in isolation can be a bit meaningless, we can use the following table to give ourselves a sense of perspective and find out how close we are to becoming an *Added Value Employee*. The example scores are just that; the key thing to focus on in the table is where your *Organisational Impact Score* sits and to note the *zone* this tends to place you in and what *type* of employee this might describe you as:

TYPE	Example Productivity Score	Example People Skills Score	Example Public Relations Score	OI Score	ZONE
KEEPERS	20	15	10	Max 1.000	**SAFE** This is the best zone to be in and where we all need to aim for. We need to score **at least** 0.420 to be here. When we're here then we really are *Added Value Employees*
	14	10	9	0.420	

CRUISERS	12	9	8	0.288
	6	5	4	0.040

STRESS
This is where the majority of people sit and the danger here is that we could end up close to the 'cut'. We need to score **at least** 0.040 to be here.

CUTTERS	4	4	3	0.016
	1	1	1	0.001 **Min**

SO LONG
This is the worst zone to be in and there is a high chance of being told to leave the organisation if we stay here.

The table shows combinations of scores for each classification and it's possible to be in the *Safe* zone by excelling at Productivity and People Skills whilst being average at PR. This is because organisational PR performance tends to lag behind Productivity and People Skills in real life.

CHAPTER 4 – THE VALUE QUESTION

The cost of keeping us falls into two categories, direct and indirect. They include:

DIRECT COSTS	INDIRECT COSTS
Salary	Employer tax and NI
Overtime	Recruitment costs
Annual bonus	Annual training costs
Pension contribution	Tools and software
Company car allowance	Telecomm costs
Other rewards	Travel and subsistence
	Office overheads
	Management overheads
	Consumables

THE VALUE QUESTION

There is a question which we have to ask ourselves, when considering our costs *and* our *Added Value Employee* Scores *and* our *Organisational Impact Score*. This question is this:

How much would you pay for you?

CHAPTER 5 – PRACTICAL OPTIONS

We always have more options than we realise. We can stop being passive and can be active instead. We can begin to solve our performance issues. Four practical options we can take to make a difference include:

- Asking for further training.
- Asking for coaching or mentoring.
- Asking to keep your role and moving to a different team.
- Asking for another role.

CHAPTER 6 – TKO TIME

We want to avoid a technical knockout, either for an act of gross misconduct, or for an act of gross stupidity. There is a comprehensive list of things *not to do* in the chapter and some of the key things to watch out for are:

1. Don't steal.
2. Don't break the law.
3. Don't bring your company into disrepute.
4. Don't break iron rules.
5. Don't break health and safety rules.

6. Don't lie on your CV.
7. Don't breach confidentiality.
8. Don't be discriminatory.
9. Don't exceed your authority.
10. Don't fall foul of substance abuse.

CHAPTER 7 – ENERGY FOR CHANGE

Any kind of change that we have to enact in order to keep our job requires *more* energy than we're currently investing in the *status quo*. This in itself is draining. Here are ten ways that clients have approached this issue and changed aspects of their lives to increase the amount of energy they bring to work with them each day:

- Date!
- Dine out.
- Play a sport.
- Play a musical instrument.
- Eat breakfast.
- Book a short break.
- Reduce your working hours.
- Join a club.
- Go to bed earlier.
- Less caffeine, more water.

CHAPTER 8 – MEASURE IT & MANAGE IT

Numbers on their own are interesting, but isolated; we need to see the trend so that we can manage our situation more effectively. Pause for a moment and look at the cartoons on the following page. Who would you rather be like?

THE DASHBOARD

A dashboard is a device that groups several performance measures in one place. When using a dashboard, the key to success is to do four things:

1. Notice if the trend lines are going down.
2. Take proactive steps to move the numbers up.
3. Seek help if you feel that you're stuck.
4. Give yourself a treat for doing well.

TYPICAL DASHBOARD

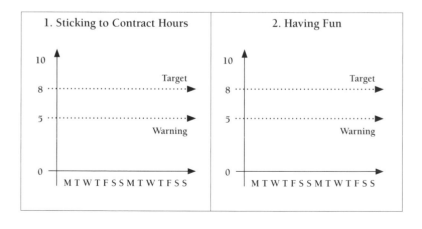

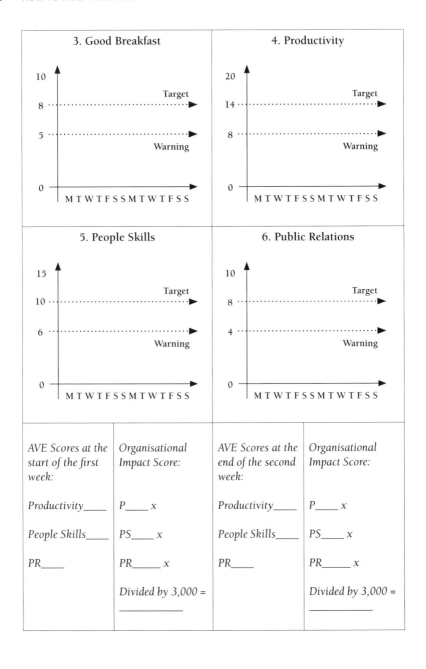

3. Good Breakfast

10

8 ··▶ Target

5 ··▶

Warning

0

M T W T F S S M T W T F S S

4. Productivity

20

14 ··▶ Target

8 ··▶

Warning

0

M T W T F S S M T W T F S S

5. People Skills

15

10 ··▶ Target

6 ··▶

Warning

0

M T W T F S S M T W T F S S

6. Public Relations

10

8 ··▶ Target

4 ··▶

Warning

0

M T W T F S S M T W T F S S

AVE Scores at the start of the first week:	Organisational Impact Score:	AVE Scores at the end of the second week:	Organisational Impact Score:
Productivity_____	P_____ x	Productivity_____	P_____ x
People Skills_____	PS_____ x	People Skills_____	PS_____ x
PR_____	PR_____ x	PR_____	PR_____ x
	Divided by 3,000 = _____		Divided by 3,000 = _____

CHAPTER 9 – PRODUCTIVITY PART 1

Contracting is a *process* and often is an *iterative process*, which means that we need to keep revisiting it until we have complete clarity. In order to make sure we have addressed all the key parts of the process, here is a 7-step approach that breaks contracting into useful chunks of activity:

7-STEP CONTRACTING PROCESS
1. Check
2. 2W+WHW
3. Competency
4. Reality Check
5. Set way-points
6. Add some contingency
7. Re-contract

CONTRACTING QUESTIONS

Often the essence of clear contracting is to ask great questions, as they promote discussion, invite people to think and unlock potential. Here are a few sample questions to get you thinking:

5 GREAT CONTRACTING QUESTIONS
1. What's your priority?
2. What is likely to cause me a problem?
3. How soon do you really need it?
4. What does success look like?
5. What are your key issues?

CHAPTER 10 – PRODUCTIVITY PART 2

Improving our productivity is about choosing to be smart with our time by focusing our efforts. Help yourself by excelling at the following and then by giving yourself a useful productivity permission:

THE 3Rs OF PRODUCTIVITY:
1. Right Quality
2. Right Quantity
3. Right Time

MAINTAIN YOUR FOCUS BY:
1. Remembering Pareto
2. Replacing 'no'
3. Producing a 4-hour list

PRODUCTIVITY PERMISSIONS:
(Here are ten samples ones, there are 35 in the chapter)

1. Good enough is good enough (beware of diminishing returns).
2. You can work first and then have some fun.
3. You can say 'not now' or 'not yet'.
4. You can put *your* priorities and needs first.
5. You can ask for help.
6. You can revisit the contract.
7. You don't have to know everything to be great.
8. You can take time to plan your work.
9. You can focus on the key tasks and improve your situation.
10. You can pace yourself (instead of leaving it all to the last minute).

CHAPTER 11 – PEOPLE SKILLS

Instead of giving ourselves a negative self-talk we need to build up our self esteem, which will enable us to excel with our People Skills.

> **PEOPLE SKILLS TIP**
> This is what we need to say when we're feeling stressed:
> - 'I have a right to be here.'
> - 'I can choose to think.'
> - 'I am a valuable person.'
> - 'I can make changes.'
> - 'I can find my voice.'

KEY COMMUNICATION SKILLS

Which ones do you do well and what are the top two areas that you need to improve on?

1. Smile with your eyes.
2. Keep your head up.
3. Keep your head straight.
4. Use the 'snow plough'.
5. Put the gun away.
6. Hold eye contact.
7. Listen with your face.
8. Make small talk.
9. Use their name.
10. Apologise if you mess up.
11. Wonder aloud.
12. Ask short questions.
13. Ask what, not why.
14. Choose relationship over task.
15. Be nice to people.
16. Use a pause button.
17. Notice fatigue.
18. Notice irritation.
19. Let it go.
20. Celebrate success.

CHAPTER 12 – PUBLIC RELATIONS

Focus your message by creating a *3-Word Strap Line*:

> ### HOW TO CREATE YOUR 3-WORD STRAP LINE
> Re-read your CV, check your last appraisal and chat with your most trusted work colleague. Review your highlights and the achievements you're proudest about and the days when you excelled. Then think about what you know you tend to do really well most of the time. What do you consider some of your key skills? What have you often been praised for? What makes you feel different, or talented? Remember that three words sound believable, whereas ten don't! Make a list of 15 words that you like and then ruthlessly cut them down until you have three which fit you the most comfortably. Examples include:
>
> - Detailed – diligent – determined
> - Friendly – thoughtful – polite

THE METROPOLITAN MODEL

A useful way to get a sense of progress in our PR activities is to reflect on the 'geographical area' we are covering in the organisation and our reach into the higher levels of seniority which exist there.

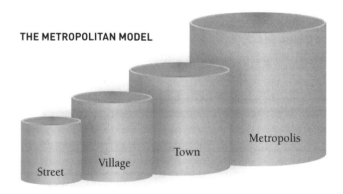

THE METROPOLITAN MODEL

Street

Village

Town

Metropolis

Street. This is your immediate environment.

Village. This is the floor you're on.

Town. This is the building you work in.

Metropolis. This is the whole organisation.

CHAPTER 13 – DEALING WITH THE 'BIG PEOPLE'

Sometimes we give our power away to the senior managers, by investing them with special abilities which they do not have. We can see the world as it is by reminding ourselves of the following truths:

> **TAKE BACK YOUR POWER**
>
> Senior managers...
> * Do not have magical powers
>
> Senior managers...
> * Need to identify and work with talented people
>
> Because...
> * Senior managers also get fired if they're no good

Taking back our power means recognising that we are just as good as the senior people in our organisation because, without us, there is no organisation. We are all worthwhile people – we all have skill and talent too, and we are all important.

CHAPTER 14 – ANCHOR NEW BEHAVIOURS

We can use anchors to keep ourselves grounded when we're stressed and to help remind us of the new things we're doing to increase our AVE scores. In Callum's case, he chose the following options and, in doing so, he kept his job.

CALLUM'S OPTIONS FOR ANCHORING IMPROVED PERFORMANCE
1. Change your desk.
2. Change your route to work.
3. Change your clothes.
4. Change your self-talk.
5. Change your grip.
6. Change something for yourself.

What would you really like to do for yourself?

CHAPTER 15 – TIME FOR MORE ACTION

Having read the book and been encouraged along the way to choose the bits that will make the biggest difference to you, take a moment to write down your top seven choices.

MY KEY LEARNING POINTS FROM *HOW TO KEEP YOUR JOB* ARE:
1)
2)
3)
4)

5)
6)
7)

Then, as a final commitment to your own future write down your next step here so that, after you put the book down, you know what you will be doing. Choose something simple and something that really appeals to you.

MY NEXT STEP IS GOING TO BE:

Well done, you have reached the end of the book!

Enjoy your career and enjoy knowing *How To Keep Your Job*.

OTHER BOOKS BY RICHARD MAUN

RICHARD MAUN

JOB HUNTING 3.0

SECRETS AND SKILLS TO SELL YOURSELF
EFFECTIVELY IN THE MODERN AGE

The secrets and skills contained in this book can make a life-changing difference to your job hunting activities because they are based on real-world experience and have been used by real people to get real jobs.

Packed with practical tips, essential tools, detailed examples and revealing the three big secrets of success, *Job Hunting 3.0* can accelerate you past the rest of your competitors and into a winning position.

To be successful in the modern world we need to know how to package our talents, how to unearth opportunities and how to assert ourselves when it matters. We need to be able to build rapport with people, talk fluently about how we can add value and be agile with our thinking in order to maximise our core strengths. We also need to use technology to our advantage and embrace the new wave of social media opportunities. Moreover, *Job Hunting 3.0* is built on process thinking, because job hunting is a sales *process* and if you set up and follow a good process, you will create opportunities for positive outcomes.

In this book you will learn about the essential elements of job hunting in the modern age, including the three-horse race, the Minute To Win It, the STAR answering technique, the demons model, the 20+ places where you can look for work, performance ratios, using numbers effectively to add value to your CV, killer questions, winning at assessment centres, the pause button, aces high and the 5-slide formula.

Job Hunting 3.0 takes us through all of these elements and more, with one goal in mind: to get you ahead of the competition so that you can secure your next job.

. . . .

Ever thought of working for yourself? Of course you have – and all the time! This is the book you wish you had ten years ago.

For many people, working for themselves is something that they yearn for and dream about. You've worked for other people's companies and been bossed around by terrible bosses for years. The time has now come to work for the best boss you could have – i.e., yourself.

This book is a straightforward, lively guide to the realities of setting up your own business, written from first-hand experience. Share in the disaster of the author's first sales meeting. Laugh at the attempts at the attempts to design a business card, and wince at the pace of learning required to stay one step ahead of clients. Through such experiences, the author reveals the secrets of developing a client base and the skills which will help you through the door to self-employment in all its bare-knuckle glory. Working for yourself is one of the richest experiences in life. This practical and inspirational book will put you on the road to success.

. . . .

Do you have a reasonable, competent, fair-minded and even-tempered boss? Congratuations! You need read no further.

Still with us? Then you are probably one of the vast majority who have problems with your manager. He or she may be difficult, temperamental, even downright brutal, but for the sake of your career (and your sanity), you have to achieve some kind of working relationship. That's where *My Boss is a B@$T@*D* comes in.

With a compelling blend of insight, wit and candour, Richard Maun dissects the personality types that make bad bosses and offers practical tips to help you survive everyday encounters with with the monster in your office. Forewarned is forearmed: once you have recognised the raw animal nature that lurks beneath that